I0798728

"Mark J Larson's *God and the Civil War: Lincoln in Moral and Theological Perspective* is an unusual integration of historical scholarship and theology. Often, historical studies ignore, suppress or are simply unaware of the pivotal role that theology and ecclesiastical convictions play in the thought and actions of people and nations. Larson's study highlights classic dialectical tensions such as God and war, American Christianity's internal conflicts, providence and responsibility, moral duty and political authority, natural law and majority rule, Lincoln the infidel attorney, and Lincoln the believing president. Here is easily readable history for discovery and debate."

— Peter A. Lillback, PhD, President and Professor of Historical Theology and Church History, Westminster Theological Seminary, Philadelphia, and author of *George Washington's Sacred Fire* and *Wall of Misconception*

"This is a very interesting, even at times provocative, book by Prof. Mark Larson. Readers will find things they like and dislike, that they will accept and not want to accept. But whatever their feelings, they will not be able to deny Dr. Larson's obvious grounding in the crucial historical-theological scholarship regarding Lincoln, God, and the Civil War. There is some fascinating material in this presentation. Readers will truly learn much about Abraham Lincoln that they never knew. The man's unique sacrificial suffering for his nation and his cause is quite moving. No American president gave his life like Lincoln did. We should be grateful to Prof. Larson for his willingness to do a theological deep dive into Lincoln that few have dared to consider."

— Paul Kengor, PhD, Professor of Political Science, Grove City College, editor of *The American Spectator*, and author of *God and Ronald Reagan*, *God and George W. Bush*, and *God and Hillary Clinton*

"Reinhold Niebuhr famously said that Abraham Lincoln's 'religious convictions were superior in depth and purity to those, not only of the political leaders of his day, but of the religious leaders of the era.' Mark Larson shows why Niebuhr was right and how Lincoln outgrew his early atheism to hold political and moral views rooted in historic Christian political and moral philosophy."

— Keith Pavlischek, PhD, and Colonel, USMC (ret.), author of *John Courtney Murray and the Dilemma of Religious Toleration*, numerous articles, and a founding editor of *Providence Magazine*

"Careful history students know that if America were to become a Bible Republic again, as it was in earlier years, this would not solve all our problems. The Bible is not read the same way in all civil and social details, even by those subscribing to the same confession. The North and the South read the same Bible and prayed to the same God, each invoking his aid against the other, Lincoln reminded everyone in his brilliant Second Inaugural Address. Our great Civil War was indeed a theological conflict, a religious war, ultimately leading to a theological crisis. Mark Larson, ably and grippingly, treats these important matters as they impact both sides of the conflict, challenging Southern verities and clearing up continuing calumnies against Lincoln. Larson helps us better understand this world, its problems, and Lincoln's remarkable place in and service to it. This is a welcome contribution to the important literature on Lincoln, the Civil War, and religion."

— Alan D. Strange, PhD, Interim President and Professor of Church History, Mid-America Reformed Seminary, and author of T*he Doctrine of the Spirituality of the Church in the Ecclesiology of Charles Hodge* and *The Imputation of the Active Obedience of Christ at the Westminster Assembly*

MARK J. LARSON

GOD AND THE CIVIL WAR

Lincoln in Moral and Theological Perspective

STONE TOWER PRESS

God and the Civil War:
Lincoln in Moral and Theological Perspective

Stone Tower Press
7 Ellen Rd.
Middletown, RI 02842
stonetowerpress.com

Paperback ISBN: 979-8-9894008-7-4

Formatting and cover design by Amy Cole, JPL Design Solutions

Cover image: *President Abraham Lincoln meeting with General George McClellan at his Antietam field headquarters 1862. Hand-colored woodcut.* North Wind Picture Archives / Alamy Stock Photo.

Printed in the United States of America

To the Memory of My Father

James Arthur Larson

Good and Faithful Servant of the Lord

and Our Beloved Son

Daniel Mark Larson

Gifted with Grace and Wisdom beyond His Years

Table of Contents

Preface

Why should we continue to give attention to Abraham Lincoln, a man from the backwoods who became the sixteenth president of the United States? This book attempts to answer the question. He was to put it simply a central figure in world history.

When did I first begin to think about the only president to have been born in Kentucky? My memory goes back to my elementary school days as a student in Almont, Michigan, and a piece of historical fiction. The boy Lincoln, I read, knew how to spell the word *Mississippi*! I was impressed. This was my first encounter with "the railsplitter." After we moved to Orchard Park, New York, my dad and I watched a movie on the tragic murder of the president and the intense manhunt for the assassin, John Wilkes Booth. Years later, there was the moving portrayal of the president in the 2012 film starring Daniel Day Lewis who claimed that he could hear the president's voice. Lincoln came to life for me.

I spent the last decade working and traveling in what had been prairie country in the nineteenth century. This was the grass-land terrain where Lincoln spent three decades as a politician and lawyer from the time that he left Indiana and then departed for the White House to take the helm of state in the time of the nation's great peril. The material culture touched me. The physical manifestations and traces of the Lincoln past drew me into the field of Lincoln studies.

A visit to the Lincoln farm in the Little Pigeon Creek Community brought me to the very place where Thomas Lincoln built an eighteen-by-twenty-foot cabin where the future president lived. My wife and I made pilgrimages to important sites in Illinois where Lincoln lived until he became president at the age of fifty-two. We strolled the grounds of the reconstructed village of New Salem along the Sangamon River where Lincoln worked as a store clerk, postmaster, and surveyor—at the same time becoming a student of law. We walked the floor of the former Illinois State Capitol building in Vandalia where Lincoln began his political career at the age of twenty-five as a member of the Illinois House of Representatives. We toured the Lincoln home at the intersection of South Eighth Street and Jackson Street in Springfield. We sauntered the campus of Knox College in Galesburg where the Fifth Debate between Lincoln and Stephen A. Douglas took place in 1858.

There have been other trips as well through the years. We sensed the wealth and refinement in the upbringing of the First Lady in a tour of the Mary Todd Lincoln House in Lexington, Kentucky. Lincoln and his wife visited her childhood home in 1847 on his way to the capital to serve a term in the United States House of Representatives. We explored the Farmington Plantation outside Louisville where Lincoln visited the boyhood home of his closest friend Joshua Speed in 1841. The three-week stay brought Lincoln face-to-face with slavery on a Southern plantation. We felt a sense of awe in a visit to Independence Hall in Philadelphia. It is the sacred ground of the American Republic, and it is one of the places where Lincoln spoke as his train headed to Washington for Inauguration Day.

A visit to the White House as a teenager was a reminder that this was the home of the renowned president. Ford's Theatre, the place of the assassination, confronted us with a sobering reminder of an unspeakably heinous crime. And what about Gettysburg? One can still almost feel the presence of the heroic men who struggled on the field of battle and the great orator and his remarkable address.

More books have been written on Lincoln than any other man in history with the exception of Jesus the Messiah. Historians consider many aspects of the president even while neglecting his political theory in relationship to mainstream Christian moral and political thought. This volume demonstrates that Lincoln's political philosophy is consistent with doctrinal positions taken by theologians and jurists in the ancient church, the medieval period, and the era from the Reformation up to the time of Lincoln.

When my dear father passed away in 2021, I found one of his treasures. It was the classic Lincoln biography written by Carl Sandburg, the two volumes of *The Prairie Years* and the four volumes of *The War Years.* My dad knew what was important in life. This book is dedicated to his memory, a man who put his trust in Jesus Christ and exemplified a life of goodness and virtue. It is also dedicated to Daniel, our beloved son, who joined his grandfather in the heavenly country in the Spring of 2024. He was so much like his grandfather whom he loved, gifted by the Holy Spirit with wisdom, able to discern the difference between good and evil, and believing in the Lord Jesus Christ, "who gave himself for our sins, that he might deliver us from this present evil age" (Galatians 1:4). What Lincoln said of his son Willie, I say of mine. Daniel was too good for this world, and therefore God called him home to the heavenly Jerusalem, the city which has foundations, whose builder and maker is God.

Introduction

The bone of contention in nineteenth-century America focused on a question of ethics. Was slavery moral or immoral? The South and its leading spokesmen—not only politicians, but significant theologians such as James Henley Thornwell, Robert Lewis Dabney, Benjamin Morgan Palmer, and Thomas Smyth—affirmed that slavery as it was practiced among them was a good thing. In the North, Abraham Lincoln along with many others believed that the institution of slavery was a grave injustice. The opponents of the American slave system at the time of Lincoln could find ammunition in the New Divinity pastors of the eighteenth century. New England men such as Samuel Hopkins and Jonathan Edwards Jr. had condemned slavery with their withering criticisms.

Lincoln was not an abolitionist.[1] In his second term of service in the Illinois legislature which met in Vandalia, he along with representative Dan Stone entered a protest on March 3, 1837, against "resolutions" which had "passed both branches of the General Assembly." Using the third person plural, Lincoln and Stone stated their position: "They believe that the institution of slavery is founded on both injustice and bad policy; but that the promulgation of abolition doctrines tends rather to increase than to abate its evils."[2] Although they identified slavery as unjust, at the same time they asserted that the Abolitionist policy was not helping matters. It was making things worse.

Lincoln identified himself as a conservative who positioned himself with the political philosophy of the Founding Fathers, which included their belief that slavery should not be extended into the territories. At the same time, Lincoln embraced the American political tradition which maintained that Americans are a Christian people who govern themselves under the providential authority of God.[3]

He consequently stood in continuity with New England theology and Old School Presbyterianism on the biblical doctrine of divine providence.

Biblical doctrine and Christian theology provided the foundation for the American Founding as reflected in the Declaration of Independence and the United States Constitution.[4] It is no surprise then that strains of thought found in Lincoln's faith, ethics, and political theory have deep roots in mainstream Christian political theology. Lincoln's thought is consistent with positions taken by theologians and jurists in the ancient church, the medieval period, and the era from the Reformation up to the time of Lincoln. We are thinking here of his reverence for the law balanced by the need to critically assess its legitimacy on the basis of natural law. Augustine and Aquinas had said the same thing. There is his position regarding the proper response to tyranny on the part of a central government. Resistance to constitutional subversion was the right thing to do. He was standing at this point in the trajectory of Calvinist resistance theory as espoused by Theodore Beza (1519–1605). At the same time, the rebellion of the South in his view had no just cause. It was therefore an instance of insurrection. This was in line with the thinking of the Genevan legal theorist Jean-Jacques Burlamaqui (1694–1748). Another example is seen in Lincoln's insistence that it is a self-evident truth that all people are created equal, and that they are endowed by their Creator with the inalienable right of liberty. Augustine and Calvin had sounded the same note that slavery was contrary to the order of nature.

The following eight chapters focus upon Lincoln in moral and theological perspective and view him in terms of the context of his contemporaries and the streams of Christian thought that flowed from the past. Chapter 1 introduces the division of opinion regarding the morality of slavery even among those who agreed about God and the way in which he governs the world. Chapters 2 and 3 place Lincoln in the context of his opponents on the slavery question and the movement to secession that resulted from the great dispute of the time. Chapter 4 presents Lincoln's effort to keep the peace even while plots were being hatched for his assassination and a spirit of rebellion had taken hold of Southern hearts. Chapters 5 and 6 survey the foundational place that the doctrine of divine providence had in American Reformed theology and in the public arena at large. Chapters 7 and 8 reflect upon Lincoln's suffering and the change that it effected in his life. We contemplate the awareness in his day that God had elevated Lincoln from the backwoods of Kentucky and Indiana to the height of political power thus effecting a great revolution, an incredible event in world history, the overthrow of slavery in the United States.

1

Moral Conduct and Divine Governance

More than fifteen thousand people had convened on the campus of Knox College in Galesburg, Illinois. The date was October 7, 1858. The weather was cold and raw. It was the Fifth Debate of three hours length between the Republican Abraham Lincoln and the Democrat Stephen A. Douglas.[1] Lincoln at six feet four inches tall with thick black hair spoke with a Kentucky accent.[2] He never gave up the pronunciation unique to his native state. He would always say things like "thar" for *there*; "Mr. Cheermun" for *Mr. Chairman*; "eddication" for *education*.[3] His high tenor voice had "carrying power" which made him audible at large gatherings.[4] Horace White with the Chicago *Tribune* attended all seven of the debates. Commenting specifically about the final debate in Alton, he noted that "Lincoln's voice" was "clear and far-reaching." He "could be heard at a greater distance than Douglas's heavy basso."[5]

Each man wanted to represent Illinois in the United States Senate. Lincoln had become a Republican, but before this he had been a Whig and thus supported the "American System" of Henry Clay, which favored a strong federal government to maintain a prosperous and stable economy.[6] Lincoln had long believed in protective tariffs and federal subsidies for internal improvements.[7] He wanted canals and railroads, and he supported a national bank.[8] He had already served four terms in the state legislature, first when it was located in Vandalia and then after it moved to Springfield.[9] He had represented Illinois for one term in the United States House of Representatives. His first election victory came in 1834 when he was twenty-five years old, an achievement which led him to borrow money so that he could purchase a tailor-made suit of clothes to wear as a new legislator. When he squared off against Douglas, he was forty-nine years of age.

Lincoln explained the essential difference between himself and Douglas on slavery, the great moral question of the day: "Judge Douglas declares that if any community wants slavery, they have a right to have it. He can say that logically, if he says that there is no wrong in slavery." Lincoln then set forth his own view: "I confess myself as belonging to that class in the country who contemplate slavery as a moral, social, and political evil."[10]

On October 13, 1858, in the Sixth Debate in Quincy, Illinois, with some twelve thousand in attendance, Lincoln elaborated and focused upon the distinction between the Republican and Democratic parties. His statements reflected his deep commitment to justice. Indeed, it was Lincoln's reason that "told him what was true or false, and therefore good or bad, right or wrong, just or unjust, and his conscience echoed back the decision." He had an "exalted sense of right and equity."[11] There is a "difference," he said, "between the men who think slavery a wrong and those who do not think it wrong." "The Republican party think it wrong."[12] He then said, "There is a sentiment in the country contrary to ours, a sentiment which holds that slavery is not wrong." "This really is the central idea of the Democratic party."[13]

The seven 1858 debates between Lincoln and Douglas and the partisan crowds that attended with their discordant views on the moral legitimacy of slavery was reflected in the divergent views of the pastors and theologians of the preceding century. It has been well said that "the trumpets" sounding from American pulpits in late 1860 and early 1861 "were producing cacophony." The cacophony revolved around the question of the Bible and slavery.[14] We need to remember as well that clashing interpretations regarding the morality of slavery extended far beyond 1860 and 1861.

We see an instance of this in 1834 at Lane Theological Seminary in Cincinnati where Lyman Beecher served as president. The students organized a series of debates over the course of eighteen days on the ethics of slavery. They came to embrace an abolitionist position. The trustees forbade further discussion on such a controversial issue. Many students protested and left for Oberlin College where they could study theology under the revivalist Charles Finney who denounced slavery as a great national sin.[15]

One may also reflect upon the eighteenth-century New England theology of Samuel Hopkins as compared with the Old School Presbyterianism of James Henley Thornwell and Thomas Smyth.[16] Hopkins insisted that there was "no way" to "bear proper testimony against this great evil but by freeing all our slaves." "This matter," he contended, "admitted of no delay, but demands our first and most serious attention and speedy reformation."[17] Slavery in America might well bring down "the righteous judgment of God." Hopkins raised this question: "Have we not all reason to fear that the vengeance of heaven will fall upon us, as a people, in ways perhaps which are not now thought of, unless we repent and reform?"[18]

Southern theologians painted a different portrait. Thornwell declared, "Slavery is not repugnant to the spirit of the Gospel." "It is one of the schools in which immortal spirits are trained for their final destiny."[19] Reverend Thomas Smyth at Second Presbyterian Church in Charleston, South Carolina, was even willing to say of the slaves: "They are healthier and happier than any other laboring class on the face of the earth."[20] The idealistic picture was that of kind masters surrounded by joyful people in bondage.[21]

The slavery question fractured the Reformed community in America in the eighteenth and nineteenth centuries.[22] Perceptive thinkers at the time worried that ecclesiastical divisions could well lead to political disunion and even war.[23] There was, however, a fundamental unity of perspective on the contours of the biblical doctrine of the providence of God.[24] As we shall see, all of the major individuals considered in this study—Jonathan Edwards, Edwards the Younger, Thornwell, Dabney, Phineas Gurley, and Lincoln himself—would have agreed with the position on divine providence outlined in the Westminster Confession of Faith (v.i): "God the great Creator of all things doth uphold, direct, dispose, and govern all creatures, actions, and things, from the greatest even to the least, by his most wise and holy providence, according to his infallible foreknowledge, and the free and immutable counsel of his own will, to the praise of the glory of his wisdom, power, justice, goodness, and mercy."[25]

This discussion draws attention to the contesting views within the Reformed community on the issue of slavery. At the same time, it demonstrates that there was a fundamental consensus regarding the features of the divine governance in the affairs of the world. Theologians from New England and among the Old School Presbyterians had the same perspectives regarding God and his relationship to history.[26]

Before we proceed, there is a question that naturally arises and which should be addressed. How shall we explain the contending views on a crucial issue of biblical ethics (the slavery question) and the essential unanimity of perspective on a fundamental article of the biblical faith (divine providence)?

The American Political Tradition

Part of the answer that helps to explain the widespread agreement regarding the divine governance over history relates to the content of the classical American political tradition. The fundamental belief of Americans was that they were a Christian people who govern themselves under the providential authority of God.[27] The biblical truth regarding the superintendence and governance of God over all things repeatedly surfaces in the symbols of the American people—one thinks, for example, of documents such as the Mayflower Compact (1620) and the Fundamental Orders of Connecticut (1639). Both statements presupposed that American colonists would govern themselves under the providential authority of God.

The Mayflower Compact began by referring to the Almighty: "*In the name of God. Amen.*" The Pilgrim signatories were here asserting that they were committed to maintaining the sacredness of the name of God. They then declared that the establishment of the new political community in Plymouth was being accomplished in the presence of the Almighty: "We, whose names are underwritten…Do by these Presents, solemnly and mutually, in the Presence of God and one another, Covenant and Combine our selves together into a Civil Body Politick."[28] The men who signed the Mayflower Compact understood that they were making a serious covenant commitment in the presence of God to set up whatever government instrumentalities would be necessary in the coming days.

The Fundamental Orders of Connecticut followed the same track, drawing attention to the concept that all historical and political events occur under the providential government of God. Providence included the fact that the people who lived in the towns constituting Connecticut resided there in accordance with the divine superintendence over all things: "It hath pleased the Almighty God by the wise disposition of his diuyne providence so to Order and dispose of things that we the Inhabitants and Residents of Windsor, Harteford and Wethersfield are now cohabiting and dwelling in and uppon the River of Connectecotte and the Lands thereunto adioyneing." The Connecticut Constitution further reflected its theocentric perspective by stating that a proper government ought to follow political principles revealed by God: "And Well knowing where a people are gathered together the word of God requires that to mayntayne the peace and vnion of such a people there should be an orderly and decent Gouerment established according to God to order and dispose of the affayres of the people."[29]

The pre-eminence of God over the political community was assumed in the founding legal documents of the new American nation and in the first public address delivered by the new American head of state. The position that the American people are dependent upon God for his blessing was included as the final sentence of the Declaration of Independence: "And for the support of this Declaration, with a firm reliance on the protection of divine Providence, we mutually pledge to each other our Lives, our Fortunes and our sacred Honor."[30] A reference to the God of Christianity was included in Article VII of the United States Constitution: "Done in Convention by the Unanimous Consent of the States present the Seventeenth Day of September in the Year of our Lord one thousand seven hundred and Eighty seven."[31] The conception that the new government would be under God appeared in the First Inaugural Address of George Washington. He publicly acknowledged God, stating that his "first official Act" as president would be the "tendering" of "homage to the great Author of every public and private good" and the offering of his "fervent supplications" that the "Almighty Being who rules over the Universe" would give his "benediction" and would "consecrate" the new "Government."[32]

This then is part of the reason for the consensus of thought within the Reformed community both in the North and South regarding the governance of God over all things in this world, including everything that happens in the political arena. The shared perspective of the New England theologians, Old School Presbyterians, and Lincoln on divine providence was very much a part of the long history of American political thought.

The Theological Basis for Doctrinal Unity and Disagreement

Even so, there is a deeper theological reason for the agreement that we have noted about God and the way in which he governs the world. There is likewise a theological basis for the disagreement regarding slavery and theological ethics among the theologians from New England and the Presbyterian Old School men from the Southern slave holding states.

John Calvin is helpful in the consideration before us. He taught that concord as to who God is and the way he governs history should be attributed to the teaching ministry of the Holy Spirit. "The Spirit," noted Calvin, "is the Master or Teacher of truth."[33] The credit for a sound doctrine of providence cannot go to "human reason," for it "neither approaches, nor strives toward, nor even takes a straight aim at, this truth: to understand who the true God is."[34] The illuminating ministry of the Holy Spirit is the ultimate reason for the harmony and shared perspective on God and providence reflected in the individuals under consideration in this study.

The disagreement on the question of the ethics of slavery ought not to be surprising. We need to remember our native fallen condition. As Calvin put it, we should not forget "the natural blindness which we brought with us from the womb." Our "walk in darkness" means that we by nature do "not distinguish between right and wrong."[35] The English theologian, William Ames, contended that even believers do not always clearly understand the nature of virtue, and specifically what is entailed in "living well in domestic economy, morality, political life," and "lawmaking," all of which "rightly pertain to theology."[36]

We also need to be realistic with respect to the outcome of biblical interpretation. Calvin reminds us, "What would otherwise be very desirable cannot be expected in this life, that is, universal consent among us in the interpretation of all parts of Scripture." "Even those who have not been deficient in their zeal for piety, nor in reverence and sobriety in handling the mysteries of God, have by no means agreed among themselves on every point; for God hath never favoured his servants with so great a benefit, that they were all endued with a full and perfect knowledge in every thing."

Calvin further stated that we should not bemoan the lack of perfect concord when it comes to the results of our biblical exegesis. He provided an explanation regarding the benefit of a lack of absolute agreement on every issue in theology. The lack of full agreement is "no doubt," said Calvin, "for this end—that he might first keep them humble; and secondly, render them disposed to cultivate brotherly intercourse."[37]

We now turn our attention in the next chapter to the clashing views of the New Divinity and Lincoln as compared with Southern Presbyterianism and Stephen A. Douglas on the slavery question. We shall then note in the succeeding chapter that the debate on the ethics of slavery was not merely an abstract philosophical debate among Christian intellectuals. It was a theological conflict that erupted in the Civil War.

2

The Question of the Ethics of Slavery

Christians in the South tended to maintain that American slavery was a perfectly Christian institution.[1] Thornwell, the theological giant from South Carolina, believed that the well-ordered society would be class-stratified.[2] Indeed, he himself was the owner of a small plantation and slaves.[3] With respect to the institution of slavery, he declared, "We cherish the institution, not from avarice, but from principle." "We look upon it as an element of strength, and not of weakness, and confidently anticipate the time when the nations that now revile us would gladly change places with us."[4] The position was that the good society, reflecting elements of the medieval feudal world, was to be found in the South.[5] Dabney, perhaps the greatest Southern theologian of nineteenth-century America, provides another example of this line of thinking.[6] When Lincoln issued the Emancipation Proclamation in 1863, Dabney held thirty-three slaves. Twenty-seven belonged to his mother, and he had six of his own.[7]

The New Divinity men did not see the issue of slavery with Southern Presbyterian eyes. Theologians such as Samuel Hopkins, Ezra Stiles, Joseph Bellamy and Jonathan Edwards Jr. were united in their opposition to American slavery.[8] They would have been able to see that the American slave institution was something much different than what God had permitted to Israel in the Mosaic law.[9] They focused upon the downside of the South's imaging of a medieval social hierarchy. The power of slave owners, they contended, was untrammeled resulting in vulgarity and even brutality.[10]

Edwards the Younger, for example, began to preach against the slave trade in the early 1770s.[11] Later, in his 1791 sermon before the Connecticut Society for the Promotion of Freedom and the Relief of Persons Unlawfully Holden in Bondage, he made the uncompromising declaration that slavery is "unjust," "wicked," and "abominable," and that it actually results in bringing injury upon the country.[12] Slavery, he argued, was contrary to natural law and biblical law, indeed, "contrary to every principle of justice and humanity."[13] He set forth similar ideas in his 1794 sermon before the governor and the Connecticut General Assembly convened at Hartford, arguing against what he believed was the great moral problem in America.[14] "To our shame, to the shame of humanity and the scandal of christianity," he lamented, "a slavery and a treatment of slaves similar to what existed among the Romans, exist and are tolerated in some parts of America."[15]

Edwards Jr. argued against the very existence of slavery on the basis of the Golden Rule articulated by Jesus in Matthew 7:12: "Therefore all things whatever ye would that men should do to you, do ye even so to them; for this is the law and the prophets." In his sermon "The Injustice and Impolicy of the Slave Trade and of Slavery," he commended two New England states: "In Massachusetts and New Hampshire, slavery is totally abolished." He then went on to say, "And if we judge of the future by the past, within fifty years from this time, it will be as shameful for a man to hold a negro slave as to be guilty of common robbery or theft." He added, "And when…slavery shall be no more; it will be an honor to be recorded in history as a society which was formed, and which exerted itself with vigorous fidelity, to bring about an event so necessary and conducive to the interests of humanity and virtue to the support of the rights, and to the advancement of the happiness of mankind."[16]

Lincoln embraced the same line of thinking espoused by Edwards Jr. and the anti-slavery New England theologians.[17] Lincoln's ancestral roots even went back to New England, the same part of the country in which the New Divinity men resided. President Lincoln was a sixth-generation descendant of Samuel Lincoln, a devoted Puritan, who arrived in Massachusetts Bay in 1637.[18] Lincoln's ethical continuity with the Edwards Jr. is reflected in a statement made by William Herndon, Lincoln's close friend and law partner for sixteen years. Herndon affirmed of Lincoln that "he approximated as nearly as human nature and the imperfections of man would permit to an embodiment of the great moral principle, 'Do unto others as ye would they should do unto you.'"[19]

The United States in the second quarter of the nineteenth century had become the largest slaveholding nation in the world.[20] Lincoln believed that American slavery was a merciless system of labor.[21] He declared, "I am naturally anti-slavery. If slavery is not wrong, nothing is wrong. I can not remember when I did not think so, and feel."[22] "Slavery is an unqualified evil to the negro, to the white man, to the soil, and to the State." "When…you have succeeded in dehumanizing the negro; when you have put him down and made it impossible for him to be but as the beasts of the field; when you have extinguished his soul in this world and placed him where the ray of hope is blown out as in the darkness of the damned, are you quite sure that the demon you have roused will not turn and rend you?"[23] In Peoria, Illinois, on October 16, 1854, Lincoln affirmed, "No man is good enough to govern another man, without that other's consent."[24] "Slavery," he said, "is founded in the selfishness of man's nature—opposition to it, in his love of justice. These principles are an eternal antagonism."[25]

Herndon commented on how Lincoln described the difference between slavery and freedom: "They are like two wild beasts in sight of each other, but chained and held apart. Some day these deadly antagonists will one or the other break their bonds, and then the question will be settled."[26]

The perpetual conflict over the morality of slavery was on display in the summer and fall of 1858 when the challenger Lincoln and the incumbent Stephen A. Douglas engaged in seven debates in Illinois in connection with the election for a seat in the United States Senate. In the First Debate on August 21, 1858, in Ottawa, Lincoln referred to "the monstrous injustice of slavery."[27]

The Lincoln-Douglas Debates

The debates in Illinois between Lincoln and Douglas are the most celebrated in American history.[28] "They were all held in the open air, on rude platforms hastily put together, shaky, and overcrowded with people."[29] They were a great sensation at the time.[30] A journalist from the New York *Evening Post,* Chester Dewey described the enthusiasm manifested at the debate in Charleston: "It is astonishing how deep an interest in politics this people take. Over long weary miles of hot, dusty prairie, the processions of eager partisans come on foot, on horseback, in wagons drawn by horses or mules; men, women and children, old and young, the half-sick just out of the last 'shake,' children in arms, infants at the maternal fount; pushing on in clouds of dust under a blazing sun, settling down at the towns where the meeting is, with hardly a chance for sitting, and even less opportunity for eating, waiting in anxious groups for hours at the places of speaking."[31] Horace White with the Chicago *Tribune* wrote about what happened after the Ottawa debate: "Half a dozen Republicans, roused to a high pitch of enthusiasm for their leader, seized him as he came down from the platform, hoisted him upon their shoulders and marched off with him, singing the 'Star-Spangled Banner.'"[32]

The debates demonstrated a profound difference between the two men on the question of what constitutes justice. Lincoln had already come to an assessment of what Douglas really believed on the basis of his support of the Kansas-Nebraska Act. Lincoln declared, "The Judge has no very vivid impression that the negro is a human."[33] The fact of the matter is that Lincoln did not truly respect Douglas as a man. The Kansas-Nebraska bill, said Lincoln, "served to prove" his "want of political conscience."[34] Throughout the debates, Douglas kept referring to the idea of popular sovereignty, "which guarantees to each state and territory the right to do as it pleases on all things local and domestic."[35] The inclusion of slavery in a new state had to be based on "the act and deed of the people."[36] A majority vote gave the institution moral legitimacy.[37]

For Douglas "justice" was nothing more than "the interest of the majority." Justice is the result of whatever side is "stronger."[38] For Douglas and legal positivism, law was nothing more than the *vox populi*.[39] Lincoln expressed the position of Douglas two months before the First Debate in his "House Divided" Speech in Springfield. Lincoln explained what popular sovereignty now meant in these memorable words: "That if any *one* man, choose to enslave another, no *third* man shall be allowed to object."[40]

Lincoln believed in the reality of natural law, that there is "a standard of right of right and wrong independent of mere opinion."[41] In his "Speech at Independence Hall" in Philadelphia on February 22, 1861, Lincoln maintained that the human rights "sentiments" expressed in the Declaration of Independence gave "hope to the world for all future time." "In due time the weights should be lifted from the shoulders of all men, and that *all* should have an equal chance."[42]

In the Seventh Debate on October 15, 1858, at Alton, twenty miles upriver from Saint Louis, Lincoln had likewise drawn attention to the Declaration of Independence and its self-evident truths, "that all men are created equal, that they are endowed by their Creator with certain unalienable Rights, that among these are Life, Liberty, and the pursuit of happiness." He stated that the Founding Fathers "meant to set up a standard for free society, which should be familiar to all, and revered by all; constantly looked to, constantly labored for, and even though never perfectly attained, constantly approximated."[43]

These unalienable rights, Lincoln argued, applied to whites and blacks.[44] No one before "Chief Justice Taney in the Dred Scott case," declared Lincoln, had ever "uttered the astounding sentiment that the term 'all men' in the Declaration did not include the negro."[45] Lincoln already contended at the First Debate in Ottawa that Douglas, by asserting a novel interpretation of the language of the Declaration of Independence, was "blowing out the moral lights around us."[46]

The Dred Scott Case

Lincoln and Douglas also dissented in their view of the Dred Scott case of 1857 in which the Supreme Court ruled that Scott as a negro was not a citizen of the United States and could not sue in federal court. In addition, the High Court determined that the Congress, as it attempted to do in the Missouri Compromise of 1820, could not exclude slavery from the territories.[47]

Lincoln expressed his understanding of the Court's decision in the Third Debate which occurred on September 15, 1858, at Jonesboro, over one hundred miles downriver from Saint Louis. Around fifteen hundred people came to hear the combatants in the small village in an area that was generally unfriendly to blacks. Lincoln said, "They reach the conclusion that, as the Constitution of the United States expressly recognizes property in slaves, and prohibits any person from being deprived of property without due process of law, to pass an act of Congress by which a man who owned a slave on one side of a line would be deprived of him if he took him on the other side, is depriving him of that property without due process."[48]

Some twelve thousand people gathered for the Fourth Debate on September 18, 1858, in Charleston on the eastern side of the state. "Judge Douglas and his friends," Lincoln argued, really wanted to "plant slavery over all the states." To remove the "slavery agitation," Lincoln and the Republican party would need to "cease speaking" of slavery "as in any way a wrong," to "regard slavery as one of the common matters of property, and speak of negroes as we do our horses and cattle."[49]

Lincoln's Perspective on Supreme Court Decisions

Lincoln believed that the mere fact that a decision was rendered by the Supreme Court did not give it moral legitimacy. He essentially positioned himself in the Ottawa Debate with President Andrew Jackson who, Lincoln noted, "did not believe in the great binding force of Supreme Court decisions."[50] In the Fifth Debate at Galesburg, Lincoln announced that he agreed with the thinking of President Thomas Jefferson that "whenever a free people should give up in absolute submission to any department of government, retaining for themselves no appeal from it, their liberties were gone."[51]

Lincoln was not impressed with the intellectual capacity and political thought of Douglas asking the question: "Has it not got down as thin as the homeopathic soup that was made by boiling the shadow of a pigeon that had starved to death?"[52] The problem with Douglas, contended Lincoln at Ottawa, was his unquestioning deference to a majority decision of the Supreme Court. "A decision of the court," Lincoln said, "is to him a 'Thus saith the Lord.'"[53]

Douglas, indeed, appeared to view the Court in the terms described by Lincoln. This is reflected in his comments at the Second Debate on August 27, 1858, at Freeport in northern Illinois, an event that drew fifteen thousand people. He castigated Lincoln and stated, "He casts an imputation upon the Supreme Court of the United States by supposing that they would violate the Constitution of the United States." He then set forth his own position: "I tell him that such a thing is not possible. It would be an act of moral treason that no man on the bench could ever descend to."[54]

In the disputation at Galesburg, Lincoln maintained that Douglas held to the Dred Scott decision "as being absolutely obligatory upon every one simply because of the source from whence it comes, as that which no man can gainsay." He levelled the charge: "He does not investigate it, and won't inquire whether this opinion is right or wrong." The problem with this approach was evident when it came to future Supreme Court decisions: "It commits him to the next decision, whenever it comes, as being as obligatory as this one."[55] Lincoln was correct in his analysis. This is where Douglas stood in his thinking. At Jonesboro, Douglas affirmed, "I have no war to make on that decision, or any other ever rendered by the Supreme Court."[56] For Douglas, as he explained at Freeport, it was "not possible" for the

Supreme Court to "violate the Constitution." The reason, announced at Galesburg, was simply that the Supreme Court is "the highest tribunal on earth."[57]

It was Lincoln, rather than Douglas, who maintained continuity with the Christian moral tradition in his realistic assessment of judges and their ethics.[58] Lincoln would not have been surprised by the observations made by Martin Bucer, appointed Regius Professor of Divinity at the University of Cambridge, during the monarchy of King Edward VI. Bucer asserted that "trials throughout the realm take place under men" who were "openly avaricious and ready to take bribes and given to other vices so that the judgments rendered by them" were "in many ways vicious and corrupt."[59]

Neither would Lincoln have demurred from the outlook of Calvin who was trained in the law schools of Orléans and Bourges. He referred to "the monstrous stupidity of judges, who can remain indifferent and unmoved in horrible confusion of civil society.[60] Lincoln could well relate to folly in the judiciary. On one occasion he referred to one of the justices on the Supreme Court as a "granny" who was so devoid of mental alacrity that "if you pointed your finger and a darning-needle toward him at the same time, he could not determine which was the sharper."[61] On the issue of integrity, Lincoln expressed his agreement with the assessment of Thomas Jefferson that "judges are as honest as other men, and not more so."[62]

A Law above the Law

Lincoln was convinced that there is a law above the law. Unlike Douglas, he refused to disregard the reality of natural law. He indeed determined to "step outside the increasing movement toward pure majoritarian process." He insisted on the reality of "a transcendent core of universal truths."[63]

Lincoln stood in continuity with positions later asserted by his younger European contemporary, the Dutch theologian Abraham Kuyper. The Christian political thinker, Kuyper argued, "is convinced that justice is not made by the statesman, but that it exists before the very notion of justice crosses his mind, and he can only approximate it in his formulation of laws."[64] The Christian political theorist further understands that there is something dreadfully wrong with human nature. There is "the reality of sin," "this awful reality."[65] Lincoln would not have dissented from this fact. He put his finger on the root problem of his time: "Slavery is founded in the selfishness of man's nature."[66] For Lincoln, the problem of human depravity meant that there is never room for an implicit faith. Rulers, including justices on the Supreme Court, cannot be blindly trusted.

Douglas and His False Accusation

The diminutive Douglas, nicknamed the Little Giant, had a reputation for engaging in fallacious reasoning, particularly *ad hominem* attacks. He was known for his ability to "scorch and smash and skewer" his opponents. Some maintain that he was "the most formidable legislative pugilist in all our history."[67] John Quincy Adams witnessed this in 1844 in a Douglas speech on the floor of the House of Representatives. Douglas spewed out "abusive invectives" and "slanders." "If his body had been made of combustible matter it would have burnt out."[68] The same kind of conduct was seen in a Douglas speech in 1858 in Havana, located on the Illinois River. Horace White of the Chicago *Tribune* witnessed what he had to say: "Douglas must certainly have been drinking before he came on the platform, because he had called Lincoln 'a liar, a coward, a wretch and a sneak.'"[69]

Douglas at Galesburg presented a false dilemma.[70] He set forth the position that there were only two options with regard to Supreme Court decisions. Douglas maintained that one could do as he did and stand by the decisions of the High Court. The only other option, what Lincoln was advocating according to Douglas, was to "resort to mob law and violence to overturn the government of laws."[71]

Lincoln's Philosophy of Law

The fact of the matter is that Lincoln rejected violence as a way of responding to erroneous Supreme Court decisions. He spoke about the Supreme Court and the Dred Scott case in Springfield on June 26, 1857. Said Lincoln, "We think its decisions on Constitutional questions, when fully settled, should control, not only the particular cases decided, but the general policy of the country, subject to be disturbed only by amendments of the Constitution as provided in that instrument itself." He then made the key statement: "More than this would be revolution."

Was there any hope for redressing a bad decision of the High Court? Lincoln believed that there was a legal remedy. He stated his position: "We think the Dred Scott decision is erroneous. We know the court that made it, has often over-ruled its own decisions, and we shall do what we can to have it over-rule this." Bad decisions can be rectified. The Supreme Court could well change its thinking and reverse its decision. Lincoln would work to that end. He then repeated the sentiment that he was committed to a legal way to achieve his objective: "We offer no *resistance* to it."[72]

Lincoln had spoken in a similar way twenty years earlier in his Address before the Young Men's Lyceum of Springfield. He had articulated a legal method of reversing illegitimate law. On the winter evening of January 27, 1838, the Lyceum met at the Second Presbyterian Church. The twenty-eight-year-old Lincoln declared, "Bad laws, if they exist, should be repealed as soon as possible."[73] At the same time, he vigorously denounced mob action and expressed his deep concern for the survival of the government in view of what he called "the increasing disregard for law which pervades the country" and "the growing disposition to substitute the wild and furious passions in lieu of the sober judgement of courts." The real danger to the survival of the country, he argued, was not from an invasion from without, but from the rise of mobocracy from within.[74] He may have had in the back of his mind the recent murder in Alton, Illinois, of Elijah

Lovejoy, a graduate of Princeton Theological Seminary, a Presbyterian minister, and an abolitionist newspaper editor.

Lincoln inculcated deep respect for the law.[75] He put it this way: "Let reverence for the law be breathed by every American mother to the lisping babe that prattles in her lap, let it be taught in schools, in seminaries, and in colleges; let it be written in primers, spelling-books, and in almanacs; let it be preached from the pulpit, proclaimed in legislative halls, and enforced in courts of justice."[76] On the other hand, the reality of the possibility of "bad laws" meant that there should not be any idea of the necessity of "absolute submission to any department of government," a situation in which there was "no appeal from it."[77]

In this delicate balance between reverence for the law and critical moral assessment of it, Lincoln stood firmly within the mainstream of Christian political thought. "The Heavenly City" which "is on pilgrimage," Augustine said, "does not hesitate to obey the laws of the earthly city by which those things which are designed for the support of this mortal life are regulated."[78] "By his own hand," Calvin proclaimed, God "has placed men in authority and in seats of justice."[79] An obligation followed from this: "Let servants obey their masters and the people their magistrates and all who dispense justice."[80] The refusal of submission, he warned, "could well imperil every government on earth."[81]

Such theological perspectives regarding the necessity of obedience to human law and government did not mean that submission was to be blind and absolute. Calvin referred to the perennial reality that there are laws that are "abhorrent not only to all justice, but also to all humanity and gentleness." How did he regard laws which are contrary to natural law, "that perpetual rule of love"? His assessment was clearly stated, "I do not think that those barbarous and savage laws" are "to be regarded as laws."[82] This was the same perspective that Thomas Aquinas had set forth in the thirteenth century. "Human law has the nature of law," he wrote, "in so far as" it "is derived from the eternal law. But in so far as it deviates from reason, it is called an unjust law, and has the nature not of law, but of violence."[83]

Lincoln in the tradition of the eighteenth-century political philosopher, Edmund Burke, believed in the reality of a transcendent moral order. Burke affirmed, "We think it necessary to declare that the laws of morality are the same everywhere, and that there is no action which would pass for an act of extortion, of peculation, of bribery, and of oppression in England, that is not an act of extortion, or peculation, of bribery, and oppression in Europe, Asia, Africa, and all the world over."[84]

The thinking of Lincoln, likewise, had continuity with Tertullian, the father of Latin Christianity. He had asserted, "What recommends a law is not the number of its years nor the dignity of its makers, but its equity and nothing else. So when laws are recognized to be unjust, they are deservedly condemned, even if they do condemn."[85]

Radically Different Perspectives

Lincoln and Douglas over the course of their seven debates had set forth two different visions of the future based on a deep divide between them touching on issues of theology, ethics, and law. Lincoln explained the difference between the two political parties in a speech that he delivered in Edwardsville just before the two men debated in Jonesboro. "The Democratic party," said Lincoln, has an attitude of "utter indifference, whether slavery or freedom shall outrun in the race of empire across to the Pacific." "The Republican party," conversely, believes that slavery is "evil," and "will use every constitutional method to prevent the evil from becoming larger and involving more negroes, more white men, more soil, and more States in its deplorable consequences."[86]

Lincoln in his "House Divided" Speech had called Douglas a "*dead lion*," or "if not a *dead* lion *for this work*, is at least a *caged* and *toothless*." He asked a question and then answered it, "How can he oppose the advances of slavery? He don't *care* anything about it. His avowed *mission is impressing* the 'public heart' to *care* nothing about it."[87] Lincoln was a very different man than Douglas. He could hardly bear up under the thought of suffering slaves. When Lincoln returned to Springfield in 1841 after visiting Joshua Speed at Farmington, the Speed mansion outside Louisville, he traveled aboard the steamboat *Lebanon* down the Ohio River. He observed twelve slaves who were "chained together." They had been separated from their wives and children and were being sold down the river. The sight, Lincoln said, brought perpetual agony to him.[88]

It is an incredible irony that on the very threshold of the Civil War, Christianity permeated American society. Protestant church buildings were everywhere. What if these houses of worship had been filled on any given Sunday in the months preceding the Civil War? It is estimated that "more than two-thirds of the nation's population would have been in attendance."[89] Americans were a Christian people. As Lincoln would put it, both North and South "read the same Bible, and pray to the same God."[90] There were, nevertheless, sharp disagreements in the land. The dispute between Lincoln and Douglas and their respective political parties regarding the ethics of slavery reflected the long-standing discord between the North and South over the same issue. The country had been moving into two alien camps over the course of several generations. The separation was at hand.

3

The Breakup of the Union

William Herndon wrote the story on Lincoln's life. Lincoln, a decade older than his colleague, selected him to be his partner even before Herndon had been admitted to the bar. Like Lincoln, Herndon had a love of learning—gathering a large library filled with volumes in history (Lecky, Buckle, and Froude); philosophy (Kant, Fichte, Feuerbach); political economy (John Stuart Mill, Henry C. Carey, Francis Wayland); and theological writers such as Ralph Waldo Emerson, Henry Ward Beecher, and Theodore Parker.[1] Herndon later reflected upon their relationship. "We never had any personal controversy or disagreement," he said. "I believe we understood each other perfectly."[2] Lincoln usually called Herndon "Billy." Herndon in turn addressed his senior partner as "Mr. Lincoln" or just "Lincoln."[3]

A Deep Loathing of Slavery

Herndon drew attention to Lincoln's second trip by flatboat to New Orleans in 1831 when the future president witnessed the evils of American slavery: "In New Orleans, for the first time Lincoln beheld the true horrors of human slavery. He saw 'negroes in chains—whipped and scourged.' Against this inhumanity his sense of right and justice rebelled, and his mind and conscience were awakened to a realization of what he had often heard and read." "Bidding his companions follow him he said, 'By God, boys, let's get away from this. If ever I get a chance to hit that thing [meaning slavery], I'll hit it hard.'"[4] Herndon affirmed, "I believe Mr. Lincoln wished to go down in history as the liberator of the black man." "Always a friend of the negro, he had from boyhood waged a bitter unrelenting warfare against enslavement."[5]

Lincoln expressed his deep emotional aversion to slavery: "I confess I hate to see the poor creatures hunted down; and caught, and carried back to their stripes and unrenewed toils." He wrote that the sight of slaves "shackled together" was "a continual torment to me, and I see something like it every time I touch the Ohio, or any other slave border."[6]

Lincoln ever looked forward to a better day. He even modelled what that day should look like in his personal interactions with black people. Elizabeth Keckly spent four years working in the White House as a seamstress for Mrs. Lincoln. She stated that the president "was as kind and considerate in his treatment of me as he was of any of the white people."[7] After Sojourner Truth visited Lincoln on October 29, 1864, she wrote, "I never was treated by any one with more kindness and cordiality than were shown to me by the great and good man, Abraham Lincoln."[8] We find the same kind of behavior on the part of the president at the White House Reception after the Second Inaugural Address on March 4, 1865. Frederick Douglass remembered what happened at the event. "As soon as President Lincoln saw me," said Douglass, "in a loud voice, so that all could hear, and looking toward me, he said, 'And here comes my friend, Frederick Douglass!'"[9]

What was Lincoln's vision of the future? In a speech delivered in 1842, he asserted, "When the victory shall be complete—when there shall be neither a slave nor a drunkard on the earth—how proud the title of that *Land*, which may truly claim to be the birth-place and cradle of both those revolutions, that shall have ended in that victory."[10] The United States did become in the course of events the land which gave birth to a great revolution, the eradication of slavery. There was going to be, as Lincoln stated at Gettysburg, "a new birth of freedom."[11] It would come, however, at a great cost.

The Apple of Discord

Lincoln did not run for political office as an Abolitionist. He reminded his fellow countrymen of this in his First Inaugural Address: "I have no purpose, directly or indirectly, to interfere with the institution of slavery in the States where it exists." He assured Southerners with these words: "I believe I have no lawful right to do so, and I have no inclination to do so."[12] His election, nevertheless, brought immediate secession.[13] His views on slavery would not be tolerated.

Indeed, Lincoln's statement in the debate with Douglas at Ottawa in 1858 foreshadowed what happened at the South Carolina secessionist convention. Lincoln had made this observation, "I leave it to you to say whether, in the history of our government, this institution of slavery has not always failed to be a bond of union, and, on the contrary, been an apple of discord and an element of division in the house." Indeed, the quarreling over the question of slavery had already erupted in a civil war in the 1850s in Kansas between those who were for slavery and those who were against it. The bloodshed in Kansas was just the beginning.

Lincoln was elected to the presidency on November 6, 1860. Six weeks later, the secessionist convention gathered at the South Carolina Institute Hall on December 20, 1860. The ultimate cause for secession was explicitly stated to be "the election of a man to the high office of President of the United States, whose opinions and purposes are hostile to slavery." The convention further declared, "He is not to be entrusted with the administration of the common Government, because he has declared that that 'Government cannot endure permanently half slave, half free,' and that the public mind must rest in the belief that slavery is in the course of ultimate extinction."[14] As James Steedman, a low-country planter in South Carolina, asserted, the "fanatics" from the North would deny the rights of Southerners, "to keep our slaves in peace & quietness."[15]

The stated reason for secession in the South Carolina convention underscores the problem with the idea of the "Lost Cause" in which many historians began to affirm that the war had been about something other than slavery.[16] Charles Hodge at Princeton Theological Seminary gave his assessment of what really happened: ""The South not only refused to enter on any course tending to the abolition of slavery, but became more and more enamored with the system; more than ever devoted to perpetuate and extend it, and at last, to accomplish this end rose up in rebellion."[17]

Benjamin Morgan Palmer's Political Sermon

What South Carolinians did in their secessionist convention was precisely what Benjamin Morgan Palmer had called for three weeks earlier in his "Thanksgiving Sermon" delivered in New Orleans on November 29, 1860.[18] Palmer, an Old School Presbyterian theologian, was a native South Carolinian and had become the pastor of the First Presbyterian Church of New Orleans in 1856. He maintained in his influential sermon that God had entrusted slavery to the South and that a "duty" had been laid upon them to conserve the institution.[19] Slavery in his view was "sanctioned in the Scriptures of God."[20] "The nature and solemnity of our present trust," he said, was "to *preserve and transmit our existing system of domestic servitude, with the right, unchallenged by man, to go and root itself wherever Providence and nature may carry it.*"

Palmer even went on to say that the South was willing to go to war to defend the right to extend slavery elsewhere.[21] "This charge we will discharge in the face of the worst possible peril," declared Palmer. "Though war be the aggregation of all evils, yet should the madness of the hour appeal to the arbitration of the sword, we will not shrink even from the baptism of fire."[22]

Palmer not only defended slavery and the right to extend it into the territories, but he also levelled charges against Lincoln and the incoming administration. He reminded his congregants of Lincoln's well-known position on the great question of the day. Indeed, in the six years following the passage of the Kansas-Nebraska Act of 1854, Lincoln delivered around one hundred seventy-five speeches about the importance of excluding slavery from the territories.[23]

"Mr. Lincoln," declared Palmer, "regards slavery as a moral, social, and political evil." He also drew to their attention the implications of a central tenet of Lincoln's political thought—that freedom, rather than slavery, ought to prevail in the territories: "The whole influence of the Executive Department of the Government, while in his hands, will be thrown against the extension of slavery into the new territories of the Union."[24]

There was nothing new about Lincoln's public policy thinking upholding the exclusion of slavery from the territories. He stood in continuity with the Northwest Ordinance of 1787, which forbade slavery in the Northwest Territory, and the Missouri Compromise of 1820, which outlawed slavery above the 36° 30' latitude line in the Louisiana Territory with the exception of Missouri, which was admitted as a slave state.[25] But there was more to it than Lincoln's embrace of two legislative acts from the early years of the Republic. The Republicans, he contended, were standing with the Founders of the government.[26] In his spellbinding Cooper Union Address in New York City on February 27, 1860, Lincoln pointed out that the first Congress passed the Ordinance prohibiting slavery in the Northwest.[27] He directly addressed the Southern people, "You say you are conservative—eminently conservative—while we are revolutionary." "What is conservatism? Is it not adherence to the old and tried, against the new and untried?" He then asserted that the Republican party stood in continuity with the Founding Fathers who did not allow slavery into the Northwest Territory: "We stick to, contend for, the identical old policy on the point in controversy which was adopted by 'our fathers who framed the Government under which we live.'"[28]

Palmer with respect to Lincoln's positions maintained that "these utterances we have heard so long." "Hitherto," he alleged, "they have come from...irresponsible men." Then with a note of sarcasm, he asserted, "But now the voice comes from the throne." "The decree has gone forth that the institution of Southern slavery shall be constrained within assigned limits."[29]

"The President elect has been chosen," Palmer declared. Dangerous implications would necessarily follow necessitating a specific course of action.[30] "The cannon of legislation," he predicted, "is to be employed in demolishing the guaranteed institutions of the South." The "Constitution" would "now be converted into an engine of oppression." "Despotism" and "tyranny" would follow.[31] Thus it was Palmer's considered judgment that secession was the only remaining option.[32] He exhorted his congregants, "Let the people in all the Southern States, in solemn council assembled...take all the necessary steps looking to separate and independent existence."[33]

While the Old School Assembly in 1861 would assert the "obligation to promote and perpetuate, so far as in us lies, the integrity of these United States, and to strengthen, uphold, and encourage the Federal Government in the exercise of all its functions," Palmer tied the South to the course of the Patriots at the time of the American Revolution.[34] He declared, "Under the rule which threatens us, I throw off the yoke of this union as did our ancestors the yoke of King George III."[35]

It Will Be a Holy War

Many theologians in the South maintained that the impending war would be a clash between the true religion of the South and the irreligion of the North. "The parties in this conflict," Thornwell wrote, are "atheists, socialists, communists, red republicans, jacobins on the one side, and the friends of order and regulated freedom on the other."[36] Palmer had the same perspective. On May 26, 1861, an Infantry Regiment of New Orleans men, known as the Crescent

Rifles, gathered at First Presbyterian Church. They would soon go forth to battle. Palmer addressed them and framed the conflict as "*an issue between religion and atheism*."[37] Around the same time, Palmer delivered a message to the Washington Artillery just prior to their departure for the scene of war in Virginia. Palmer stood on the steps of the portico of the City Hall in New Orleans. Five thousand citizens were also present to hear his address. He told the soldiers that they were "the gallant defenders of a holy cause."[38]

Many Reformed believers at the time would have vigorously dissented from this explanation of unfolding events. "Resolutions of support" for the Union cause "came from the Philadelphia Presbytery of the Reformed Presbyterian Church in North America."[39] An ascription of atheism to Presbyterians with Scottish roots would have been deeply offensive.[40]

Presbyterian theologians were not the only ones to regard the Civil War as a war of religion. Reverend O. S. Barten, the rector of St. James Church in Warrenton, Virginia, preached a sermon on June 13, 1861, in which he sharply distinguished between the North which was "run by infidels and fanatics under a godless government" and the South consisting of "Christian men in a Christian government presiding over a Christian people."[41] Later on, a preacher from Tennessee named Jesse Cox asserted that the Union army was "anti-christ, the Beast that" is to "assend from the bottomless pits."[42] George R. C. Todd, the brother of Lincoln's wife, sided with the Confederacy and maintained that the war was between the "children of the devil" and the "children of the Lord."[43]

The North had the declaration "In God We Trust" placed on its two-cent coin, while the Confederate States asserted their belief that God would be their defender by placing the Latin expression "Deo Vindice" on it seal. Such declarations prompt us to remember that soldiers on both sides were impacted by the Second Great Awakening and by the revivals that broke out in Northern camps and in the Army of Northern Virginia and the Army of Tennessee.[44] Such affirmations were likewise an echo of the English Civil War in which

King Charles I described his opponents as "Brownists, Anabaptists and Atheists," and the Parliamentarians flew battle standards with inscribed statements such as "Verbum Dei," "Sacra Scriptura," and "Jehova Nisi."[45]

Palmer even recalled the memory of Cromwell who manifested the Crusade mentality when he massacred Irish combatants and noncombatants alike at Drogheda. Palmer assured the soldiers, "We have no doubt of the part which will be assigned you to play; and when we hear of your cannon echoing from the mountain passes of Virginia will understand that you mean, in the language of Cromwell at the Castle of Drogheda, 'to cut this war to the heart.'"[46] Thomas Smyth likewise rehearsed the inspiring vision of Cromwell's soldiers "who passed from the prayer meeting to the field of battle, with their Bibles girt under their armour."[47]

Slaughtering Prisoners of War

The American Civil War was to be a holy war.[48] This was how Stonewall Jackson viewed it. He wanted to follow the holy war guidelines of the Old Testament and advocated a policy of taking no prisoners. The general declared, "We ought to meet the Federal invaders" and "raise at once the black flag, viz., 'No quarter to the violators of our homes and firesides.'" "The Bible," he said, "is full of such wars."[49] Confederate soldiers under the command of Nathan Bedford Forrest acted out this line of thinking following the capture of Fort Pillow located on the Mississippi River. They slaughtered over two hundred Federal soldiers after they had surrendered.[50] This was not an isolated event. In the last two years of the war, Confederates massacred Union soldiers, black and white, in every theater of the conflict.[51]

Lincoln did not approve of this mentality and behavior.[52] "Civilized belligerents," he said, "do all in their power" to "hurt the enemy, except a few things regarded as barbarous or cruel. Among the exceptions are the massacre of vanquished foes, and noncombatants, male and female."[53]

Lincoln, rather than General Jackson, stood in continuity with the teaching of Calvin at this point.[54] Calvin recognized that God had given a command to the Jews to annihilate the Canaanites: "It is true a special command was given to the ancient people to destroy the nations of Canaan." However, Calvin went on to say, "To us, in the present day, no certain region marks out our precise boundaries; nor are we armed with the sword to slay all the ungodly."[55] "Even in lawful wars," said Calvin, "cruelty is to be repressed, and bloodshed is to be abstained from as much as possible." "God would have his people" to be "mindful of humanity in the very midst of the din of arms."[56]

Enemies who laid down their arms in battle and who appealed for mercy should be spared. This was the view of Calvin. He spoke against the slaughter of captives by asking his congregation two questions: "What a thing then is it, when men shalbe put all to the sworde without sparing? Is it not as good as a defying of God?"[57]

Calvin possibly had in mind the widespread practice in the Middle Ages of victorious knights massacring peasant infantry.[58] Or he may have been thinking of the Ottoman Turks and the Sultan's disregard of any commitment to the justice in war practice of restraint in battle as seen at Mohacs in Hungary in 1526. Suleiman's policy of taking no prisoners resulted in the annihilation of some 30,000 soldiers. The captives which he temporarily held were put to death. Suleiman recorded the following in his diary entry for August 31, 1526: "The emperor, seated on a golden throne, receives the homage of the vizirs and beys: massacre of 2,000 prisoners: the rain falls in torrents."[59]

Calvin's response to the slaughter of captive soldiers was straightforward—putting all the captives to death would be to flout God himself.

Ministers Taking Up the Sword

The conflict would be a war of religion.[60] Southern and Northern ministers with this perspective left their pulpits for the battlefield. They did not sign up to serve as chaplains, but rather as combat soldiers. There was, in fact, a shortage of chaplains in both armies, North and South.[61] A few examples may be cited. Mark Lowrey, a Baptist pastor in northern Mississippi stopped preaching in 1862 and organized the Thirty-second Mississippi and was elected colonel. Significant numbers of Methodist preachers became combat soldiers in the Confederate army. The same thing happened in the North. Sixty Methodist ministers from Illinois volunteered to fight after the Battle of Bull Run.[62] A Methodist minister from New York, a sharp shooter named Lorenzo Barber, shot and killed enemy combatants in various engagements.[63] The Seventy-third Illinois had so many ministers that it was called the "Preacher Regiment."[64]

Some of the ministers who took up the sword were significant theologians. One of the most famous clerics was Leonidas Polk, the "Fighting Bishop." Polk, a slave owner, had served as bishop of Louisiana and founded the University of the South. He believed that it was his duty as a bishop to take up arms and served as a major general for the Confederates, seeing action in memorable battles at Shiloh and Chickamauga. Another well-known minister who joined the military conflict was the Presbyterian theologian Robert Dabney. Initially, in 1861, he joined the army commanded by General Pierre Beauregard and served for four months as a chaplain with the 18th Virginia Volunteers. He could write about seeing "the puffs of smoke mount up from opposing cannon," and "the bayonets of the enemy gleam as their columns advanced."[65] In 1862, Dabney became a combatant when he accepted the offer of General Thomas Jackson to serve as Adjutant-General of his army. This position meant that Dabney became Jackson's secretary and accompanied him in all his movements, marches, and battles.[66]

It should be noted that Thomas Aquinas, the preeminent medieval theologian, had argued that it was not lawful for ministers to fight. He referred to two problems with pastors taking up arms and going off to war. In the first place, "warlike pursuits are altogether incompatible with the duties of a bishop and a cleric." "Warlike pursuits," said Aquinas, "hinder the mind very much from the contemplation of Divine things, the praise of God, and prayers for the people." In addition, the killing of enemy soldiers by a minister was unseemly: "It is unbecoming for them to slay or shed blood, and it is more fitting that they should be ready to shed their own blood for Christ."

There was, however, a way for pastors to help with the prosecution of a just war. "Prelates and clerics may," Aquinas contended, "take part in wars, not indeed by taking up arms themselves, but by affording spiritual help to those who fight justly."[67]

Aquinas was explicitly clear in his teaching. Holy war advocates, nevertheless, distanced themselves from such perspectives. The First Crusade had been proclaimed by Pope Urban II in 1095 to liberate Jerusalem from Muslim control and oppression. The crusade mentality continued into the sixteenth century. A crusade league—including not only Spain and Venice, but also the Papacy—defeated the Turks in the Battle of Lepanto on October 7, 1571.

Martin Luther spoke strongly against the medieval holy war tradition. "The pope and the bishops," he said, "would be destroying their calling and office to fight with the sword against flesh and blood. They are not commanded to do this; it is forbidden."[68] Luther focused upon the head of the Catholic Church: "It is not right for the pope" to "lead a church army."[69] He denounced two contemporary popes, Julius II and his "arms" and Clement VII, "who people think is almost a god of war."[70] Luther had no use for the crusade ideology in which "the pope, along with his followers, wages war."[71]

Reformed political thought likewise frowned upon the idea of ministers going off to war with the intention of killing. Huldrych Zwingli, for example, in Article 36 of *An Exposition of the Articles* affirmed that the office of a minister is to teach the Word of God.[72] Rulers, on the other hand, "look after the office of the sword."[73] Zwingli addressed the pope who wanted to take up arms against the Ottoman Turks who were threatening Europe. Zwingli exhorted, "Listen to Christ, oh pope, 'Put it away'"—referring here to the sword. "The secular princes," he said, "are undoubtedly quite capable of protecting their own land." He then added, "Take no other sword into your hand than the sword of the Spirit which is the word of God."[74]

Zwingli, of course, was not entirely consistent with his own teaching. We see this in 1531 when five Catholic cantons declared war on Zürich. A small Zürich force of two thousand men confronted a larger Catholic army of eight thousand near Kappel on October 11. Zwingli joined the Zürich forces as a chaplain. He had taught in continuity with Thomas Aquinas that ministers ought not to wield the sword, but he decided in the emergency of the moment to take up the sword and to fight alongside his soldiers. He died in the bloody engagement that lasted less than an hour.

The Rapid Succession of Events

Events moved quickly following the election of Lincoln to the presidency on November 11, 1860. Palmer and the advocates of secession soon responded in the weeks following the election. Slavery, they argued, was a divine and holy institution, a good thing for the masters and a good thing for the slaves. The South had a biblical and moral right to transmit the institution of slavery wherever God opened the door for them to do so. They assumed that Lincoln would rule as a tyrant and would destroy slavery and the Southern economy. He was a monster who would "free the slaves by gunpoint."[75] Since despotism was sure to come, the South was compelled to secede to protect its way of life and to avoid being contaminated by the ungodly from the North.

War was sure to follow. It would be a conflict in many Southern eyes between the atheists of the North and the Christians of the South. A war of religion would descend at times into a take-no-prisoners approach in battle. Holy war meant that ministers, Union and Confederate, would leave their preaching for slaying the enemy on the field of battle.

4

Endeavoring to Keep the Peace

The fundamental assumption of Benjamin Morgan Palmer and many others was that Lincoln's moral and theological commitments made him an unlawful ruler. This meant that obedience was not necessary.

Palmer's position, however, was out of accord with mainstream Christian political thought. Theodore Beza, the first rector of the Academy in Geneva, stressed that legitimate political rulers have always served by virtue of the election of the people.[1] The people bestow authority upon the magistrates. "The authority of all magistrates," he argued, "however supreme and powerful they be, is dependent upon the public authority of those who have raised them to this degree of dignity."[2] "Nature itself seems to proclaim" this concept "with a loud voice."[3] Beza provided historical proof for a theory that was essentially self-evident. He asserted that his thesis "may be corroborated by the history of nearly all nations."[4] He argued that in every state and under every form of government the people elect their rulers.[5]

Lincoln as a Legitimate Ruler

Lincoln was not a usurper. On November 6, 1860, he had defeated the three other presidential candidates—the Southern Democrat

John C. Breckinridge, the Democrat Stephen A. Douglas, and the Constitutional Union candidate John Bell. There was nothing illegal about Lincoln's elevation to the presidency. He did not seize power. He was put into office by the vote of the people. He had garnered 187 votes in the Electoral College. His three opponents had acquired a total of 123 electoral votes.[6] The people had chosen him to be the chief magistrate in the American republic.

The United States was a republic. As Lincoln put it, the nation had a fundamental commitment to "government of the people, by the people, and for the people."[7] Significant implications followed from this fact. For one thing, a republic was to be valued and protected. As John Calvin noted, "a well-constituted republic is a singular benefit of God."[8] Lincoln would have agreed with the reformer's statement that "in this especially consists the best condition of the people, when they can choose, by common consent, their own shepherds."[9] Furthermore, once a people have made their selection, they have a moral obligation to uphold those whom they have chosen to office. We are to submit, Calvin insisted, to him who is "a father of the country" and a "shepherd of his people."[10]

Christian political philosophy had even maintained that submission was to be given to him who is lazy, careless, pleasure seeking, corrupt, avaricious, oppressive, and sacrilegious.[11] Public obedience must be shown even to him who is "very wicked" and "utterly unworthy of all honor."[12] The people must submit themselves regardless of the kind of government under which they find themselves.[13]

The determinative biblical text was Romans 13:1–2, a command given to believers in the days of the Roman empire: "Let every soul be subject unto the higher powers. For there is no power but of God; the powers that be are ordained of God. Whosoever, therefore, resisteth the power, resisteth the ordinance of God; and they that resist shall receive to themselves damnation." To rebel against "a duly constituted, legally operating civil government" was a serious moral offence with dreadful consequences. The Southerners in much Union thinking had violated the command of God.[14]

The Confederates were also out of step with the Christian moral tradition. "Divine providence," Calvin wrote, "has wisely arranged that various countries should be ruled by various kinds of government." What posture should citizens take in all circumstances? "It is our duty to show ourselves compliant and obedient to whomever he sets over the places where we live."[15] There was nothing unusual about Calvin's teaching. John of Salisbury in the twelfth century had declared, "Loyal shoulders should uphold the power of the ruler." He furthermore stated, "Inferiors should cleave and cohere to their superiors, and all limbs should be in subjection to the head."[16]

Plotting to Kill Lincoln

Calls to loyalty, though, went unheeded. Seven states announced their separation from the Union. Secession was one thing, but recourse to violence was another. Conspirators plotted to assassinate the president-elect as he passed through Baltimore on his way to the District of Columbia for the inauguration. In what is now the town of Perryman, a militia of Southern sympathizers had been drilling with the intention of killing Lincoln.[17] Assassins hoped to strike when he was in his railroad carriage between the two stations in Baltimore. Government officials in Baltimore showed no interest in offering protection for Lincoln. He was, however, accompanied by two bodyguards, Allan Pinkerton and Ward Hill Lamon. Taking every precaution, Lincoln traveled in the middle of the night. His train arrived at Baltimore around 3:30 in the morning and finally headed south to the capital around 4:30.[18]

The aspiring assassins of the president-elect were apparently oblivious to the wide ethical implications of David's refusal to take the life of King Saul when he had the opportunity to do so. 1 Samuel 24:10 provides David's determination: "I will not put forth mine hand against my lord; for he is the LORD's anointed." They essentially set themselves against Christian moral theology and its solemn warnings against this course of behavior. Thomas Aquinas in the thirteenth century had called attention to the deleterious consequences that would follow from the mentality that assassins may take out political figures with whom they disagreed: "Should private persons attempt on their own private presumption to kill the rulers, even though tyrants, this would be dangerous for the multitude as well as for their rulers." He reasoned, "This is because the wicked usually expose themselves to dangers of this kind more than the good, for the rule of a king, no less than that of a tyrant, is burdensome to them." "Consequently, by presumption of this kind, danger to the people from the loss of a good king would be more probable than relief through the removal of a tyrant."[19]

The medieval mind took the threat uttered by Jesus in Matthew 26:52 with utter seriousness: "All they that take the sword shall perish with the sword." The forbidden action of taking up the sword meant, as Augustine said, "to use weapons against a man's life, without the sanction of the constituted authority."[20] The threat itself, contended Aquinas, should be understood on two levels, the literal and the metaphorical. For Aquinas, Jesus' statement applied not only to this life, but also to the next: "And yet even those who make sinful use of the sword are not always slain with the sword, yet they always perish with their own sword, because, unless they repent, they are punished eternally for their sinful use of the sword."[21]

Lincoln's First Inaugural Address

It was in the context of secession with Southern emotions running high that Lincoln delivered his First Inaugural on March 4, 1861. The seven states which had seceded already had met in Montgomery, Alabama, and formed the Confederate States of America on February 8, 1861.[22] This was to be expected. Augustine noted that there is a connection between sedition and confederation: "Even in the extreme case when" men "have separated themselves from others by sedition, they cannot achieve their aim unless they maintain some sort of semblance of peace with their confederates in conspiracy."[23]

Federal property in South Carolina, Georgia, Alabama, Mississippi, Louisiana, and Florida had already been seized.[24] As Lincoln later summarized developments, "A disproportionate share of the Federal muskets and rifles had somehow found their way into these States, and had been seized to be used against the Government. Accumulations of the public revenue, lying within them, had been seized for the same object."[25] The Confederates were getting ready for war, even though similar war-like preparations were not being made on the Union side.[26]

In the context of hysterical claims of presidential tyranny and escalating belligerence, Lincoln patiently made every effort to keep the peace.[27] He announced that he had no legal right to interfere with slavery in the states where it existed.[28] He endeavored to calm all fears. He gave the assurance that "the prosperity, peace, and security of no section are to be in any wise endangered by the new incoming Administration."[29] He insisted, "There will be no invasion, no using of force against or among the people anywhere."[30]

Lincoln concluded with an appeal to the South: "We are not enemies, but friends. We must not be enemies. Though passion may have strained it must not break our bonds of affection."[31] Such words demonstrate that Lincoln was putting into practice what he had long before advised in Springfield on February 22, 1842. "If you would win a man to your cause, *first* convince him that you are his sincere friend."[32]

It is incredible that many southerners viewed Lincoln's First Inaugural not as conciliation, but provocation. The Charleston *Mercury* labelled the speech as a declaration of war.[33] Lincoln on a later occasion set forth the course of action that he had outlined in his First Inaugural: "The policy chosen looked to the exhaustion of all peaceful measures, before a resort to any stronger ones. It sought only to hold the public places and property not already wrested from the Government." "It promised a continuance of the mail, at Government expense, to the very people who were resisting the Government."[34]

There was nothing new about many of the president's statements delivered on March 4, 1861. It was classic Lincoln. It echoed remarks made at Independence Hall a week and a half earlier: "There is no need of bloodshed and war." "There will be no blood shed unless it is forced upon the Government."[35] The First Inaugural reflected the contents of a letter that he had sent to his friend Joshua Speed in which he acknowledged that Speed had a "legal right to the slave." He stated, "I am not aware that *any one* is bidding you yield that right, very certainly *I* am not. I leave that matter entirely to yourself." At the same time, Lincoln stated, "I do oppose the extension of slavery, because my judgment and feelings so prompt me."[36]

The Question of Secession

The Constitution does not leave an absolutely clear answer on the issue of the permanence of the Union.[37] This remains a controversial question to this very day.[38] Had the states given up their sovereign rights and merged their identities forever? Or was the Union such that the states could withdraw at any time?[39] Lincoln had a decided position on this question of giving primacy to the center or the periphery, the whole or the parts.[40] For him the Union and not the states was central. On one occasion, he provided a witty perspective concerning those who stressed the primacy of the states over the federal government. With respect to "state sovereignty," he said, "Advocates of that theory always reminded [me] of the fellow who contended that the proper place for the big kettle was inside of the little one."[41]

Lincoln insisted that the American people are one nation. He was a "fervent nationalist" when many Americans at the time were "aggressive localists."[42] Lincoln, in fact, believed that the planter aristocracy was behind the secession movement and that it did not represent the Southern people who were Union loyalists.[43] In his view secession was not legal: "In legal contemplation the Union is perpetual." "No State," he declared, "upon its own mere motion can lawfully get out of the Union."[44] Already on December 13, 1860, Lincoln had declared, "The right of a state to secede is not an open or debatable question. It was fully discussed in Jackson's time and denied not only by him, but by vote of Congress."[45] In his view, the secession argument was deceptive, "an ingenious sophism" concocted for the purpose of sugar coating a spirit of rebellion.[46] He accordingly addressed the South with the expression "my dissatisfied fellow-countrymen."[47]

At the same time, Lincoln acknowledged that there may be occasions when subjects may take up arms against a central government in the case of constitutional subversion.[48] He conceded, "If by the mere force of numbers, a majority should deprive a minority of any clearly written constitutional right, it might in a moral point of view justify revolution; certainly would if such right were a vital one."[49] The federal government, however, had not undermined constitutional rights. Lincoln stated, "But such is not our case." He raised a question and gave an answer: "Is it true, then, that any right plainly written in the Constitution has been denied? I think not."[50]

The Bombardment of Fort Sumter

The issues facing the country were serious indeed. Lincoln underscored that fact in the First Inaugural. "In your hand and not mine," he said, "is the momentous issue of civil war." He gave a promise: "The Government will not assail you." He explained the facts of the case: "You can have no conflict without being yourselves the aggressors."[51]

Aggression was the choice, and the conflict came. The fundamental perspective of the South was that an independent nation could not allow a foreign port in one of its harbors.[52] The United States refused the demand of Southern leaders to transfer Fort Sumter to the Confederacy. President Jefferson Davis responded with the fateful command. Charleston's cannons opened fire. The date was April 12, 1861. The war had begun.[53]

Lincoln had a long-standing concern about the necessity of a just cause as a justice of war requirement. He believed, for example, that the Mexican War had no just cause.[54] The war against Mexico in his view was an instance of "unprovoked aggression" on the part of the United States "against a feeble neighbor for territorial gain."[55]

Lincoln contended, though, that the Civil War was a very different thing. He explicitly stated that the making of war by the United States on the Confederacy had a just cause. There had been an act of unprovoked aggression, and military force was therefore being used to suppress the rebellion. Before Ulysses S. Grant and the Army of the Potomac crossed the Rapidan in the spring of 1864, Lincoln wrote a letter to his new Lieutenant General in which he said, "If there is anything wanting which is within my power to give, do not fail to let me know it. And now, with a brave army and a just cause, may God sustain you."[56]

Lincoln in all of this reflected longstanding Christian political thought on the issues of tyranny, the relationship between a central government and inferior magistrates, and a just cause for war. The famous eighteenth-century professor of jurisprudence at the University of Geneva, Jean-Jacques Burlamaqui, had taught that "when subjects take up arms against their prince, they either do it for just reasons" or "without a just and lawful cause." "In the latter case," he contended, "it is rather a revolt or insurrection."[57] A just cause for taking up arms against a central government would be tyranny. In the event of tyranny, when a sovereign "injures his subjects" and "subverts the fundamental laws," the people "have a right to resist their sovereign," "a right to rise against him, and even to deprive him of the supreme power."[58] "The people," contended Burlamaqui, ought not to be understood as "the vile populace or dregs, of a country, but the greatest and most judicious parts of the subjects."[59]

Beza had set forth similar ideas in the sixteenth century regarding the proper response to tyranny on the part of the inferior magistrates, which he identified as intermediate authorities between the supreme magistrate and the people.[60] He stated, "All magistrates are obliged to thwart tyranny on an interim basis by defending persons within their jurisdiction against the unjust exercise of authority by the central authority."[61] Such a defense would necessarily entail the taking up of arms. Resistance, he argued, was the duty of inferior magistrates in the face of tyranny when political figures in the central government undermined established law—in the context of "authority setting itself against the laws," in a setting in which the central government "strives with might and maim to subvert the constitution."[62]

Lincoln in continuity with Calvinist political thought understood that constitutional subversion would be a just cause for resistance on the part of the states. He maintained, though, that the federal government had respected all the constitutional rights of the slave-holding states. He fully understood that under the Constitution he had "no lawful right" to "interfere" with slavery in the states where it already existed.[63] There was not, therefore, a just cause for the bombardment of Fort Sumter.[64]

From Lincoln's perspective, the shelling of Fort Sumter was a hasty and ill-considered attack. It was likewise so from the standpoint of the established principles of Reformed political thought. Beza had qualified his call to armed resistance with three axioms. First, "the tyranny must be undisguised and notorious." Secondly, "recourse should not be had to arms before all other remedies have been tried." Thirdly, there should not be the taking up of arms "before the question had been thoroughly examined, not only as to what is permissible, but also as to what is expedient, lest the remedies prove more hazardous than the very disease."[65] Words of caution had been set forth in influential political treatises, but long-standing wisdom went unheeded.

The Sin of Sedition

Lincoln explicitly defined what an act of violence against the United States would entail. Raising arms against the Federal government would be an insurrection.[66] To use the language of medieval theology, Aquinas had stated, "Sedition, in its proper sense, is between mutually dissentient parts of one people, as when one part of the state rises in tumult against another part." "Sedition," he said, "is contrary to the temporal unity of the multitude, for instance of a city or a kingdom." It was an act with serious moral implications: "Since sedition is opposed to a special kind of good, namely the unity and peace of a people, it is a special kind of sin."[67]

Calvin warned against sedition in the strongest terms. "Let no man deceive himself here," he warned. "For since the magistrate cannot be resisted without God being resisted at the same time, even though it seems that an unarmed magistrate can be despised with impunity, still God is armed to avenge mightily this contempt toward himself."[68]

Lincoln likewise believed that the man who participated in an insurrection had great moral culpability. On one occasion, a woman from Baltimore appealed to the president in behalf of her son who had joined the Confederate forces and was now in a federal prison. Lincoln said to her, "And now that he is taken prisoner, it is the first time, probably, that you have ever shed tears over what your boy has done. Good morning, Madam, I can do nothing for your boy today."[69]

The same perspective embraced by Lincoln was articulated by Reverend George Junkin, Stonewall Jackson's first father-in-law. Reverend Junkin was an Old School Presbyterian who served as president of Washington College in Lexington, Virginia. The Reverend regarded secession as "the essence of all immorality." When Virginia decided to leave the Union Junkin identified the action as "a rebellion without a cause."[70]

Suppressing the Rebellion

Lincoln no doubt would have nodded in agreement with such positions on sedition coming from medieval and Reformation theology and restated in his own time. This was why he called for 75,000 soldiers to serve for three months, referring to "the Rebellion" and stating that he was attempting "to suppress the rebellion by force of arms."[71] At the same time, he had to respond to enemies from within the United States. As soon as the Civil War began, Confederate sympathizers in Maryland sabotaged the federal government destroying telegraph and railroad lines. Lincoln, as commander-in-chief, affirmed, "I suppose I have a right to take any measure which may best subdue the enemy."[72] Fearing that the civil courts would not convict the saboteurs, Lincoln on April 27, 1861, suspended the writ of habeas corpus between Philadelphia and Washington, D.C.

Sir William Blackstone, the eighteenth-century English jurist, had spoken about the suspension of the writ of habeas corpus in England. He maintained that when the state is in danger the writ may be suspended by Parliament alone and not by the executive power. Lincoln, though, believed that Blackstone was not operating in a context where the Parliament was not in a position to act.[73] The United States Congress was not in session when Lincoln suspended the writ. Lincoln, furthermore, appealed to Art. 1, Sec. 9, of the Constitution: "The Privilege of the Writ of Habeas Corpus shall not be suspended, unless when in Cases of Rebellion or Invasion the public Safety may require it."[74] The president declared, "We have a case of rebellion," and "the public safety does require the qualified suspension of the writ."[75] Chief Justice Roger Taney maintained that Congress alone could do this because this provision is in Article 1 of the Constitution. Lincoln disregarded his opinion.

"We must," said Lincoln, "settle this question now, whether in a free government the minority have the right to break up the government whenever they choose."[76] The attack on Fort Sumter meant that the great ethical and political questions of the day would be settled on the field of battle. The contending parties would engage in what many viewed as a war of religion between two alien camps in which there was widespread agreement that God is the supreme governor of all events in history. Lincoln, as we shall see in the next chapter, stood firmly within the trajectory of Calvinist thought on divine providence as articulated by New England divines and Old School Presbyterians of the South.

5

The Providence of God in Reformed Theology

The nineteenth-century reflected profoundly different perspectives on the question of the morality of slavery. Much of the divergent political thought flowed from the fundamental disagreement regarding the ethics of enslavement. Against this background of a deep-seated division of thought resulting in the Civil War, there was a remarkable continuity of perspective on the matter of divine providence as reflected in the leading representatives of the New England theology and Old School Presbyterianism.

There was no division on providence between Jonathan Edwards and his son Jonathan Jr. representing New England Congregationalism and Thornwell, Dabney, and Gurley of the Old School Presbyterian camp. Each theologian drew attention to a number of ideas related to divine providence. They maintained that God superintends all events in history and the political arena—such that God establishes in the sphere of fallen humanity specific governments and raises up statesmen to bless many of the nations. Each nation, they maintained, will experience the blessing of God following repentance, while the chastening of God will most certainly come in response to rampant sin and impenitence. Even more amazing is the fact that these positions were embraced and explicitly articulated at the highest level of the government of the United States in the thinking of President Abraham Lincoln.

Lincoln and Samuel Hopkins

The perspective that governments conduct their business and that nations live under the watchful eye of God showed itself on the national stage in the speeches of Abraham Lincoln. In his Second Inaugural Address Lincoln contemplated the Civil War and maintained that it was a manifestation of the judgment of God upon the sins of the American people. Lincoln essentially reaffirmed the position of Samuel Hopkins, the New Divinity theologian who witnessed the slave trade while serving as a pastor in Newport, Rhode Island. Hopkins anticipated what would happen if Americans refused "to put away the holding" of "the African in slavery." He asked, "Have we not the greatest reason to fear, yea, may we not with great certainty conclude, God will yet withdraw his kind protection from us, and punish us yet seven times more?"[1]

Lincoln sounded the same note on March 4, 1865, in his Second Inaugural Address. He declared, "If we shall suppose that American slavery is one of those offenses which, in the providence of God, must needs come, but which, having continued through his appointed time, he now wills to remove, and that he gives to both North and South this terrible war, as the woe due to those by whom the offense came, shall we discern therein any departure from those divine attributes which the believers in a living God always ascribe to him?" Even if the "mighty scourge of war" should continue indefinitely, Lincoln professed this faith: "The judgments of the Lord are true and righteous altogether."[2]

In his fundamental beliefs regarding the biblical doctrine of providence, Lincoln articulated positions that were at the center of the worldview of leading New England Congregationalists and Old School Presbyterians in the South. We find that Lincoln's ideas on divine providence were not unusual. The Senior Edwards and Edwards Jr. had affirmed similar positions. Essentially the same teaching reappeared in the thought of Thornwell in South Carolina and Dabney in Virginia.

The Teaching of Jonathan Edwards

Jonathan Edwards reinforced the longstanding providential view of history that had existed in the American colonies from the seventeenth century onward. Adverse events in the political community, he maintained, should be directly traced to divine judgment. In his sermon "A Strong Rod Broken and Withered" delivered on the occasion of the death of John Stoddard, the renowned statesman of Massachusetts, he asserted, "The removal of such rulers from a people by death is to be looked upon as an awful judgment of God on that people, and is to be greatly lamented."[3] He counseled, "The awful voice of God in this providence is worthy to be attended to by this whole province, and especially the people of this country, but in a more peculiar manner by us of this town." Stoddard's death led to an inescapable conclusion: "We have now this testimony of the divine displeasure, added to all the other dark clouds God has lately brought over us, and his awful frowns upon us." Stoddard's passing, Edwards affirmed, was not an accident. It was "an awful manifestation of his supreme, universal and absolute dominion, calling us to adore the divine sovereignty."[4]

Edwards's sermon portrays the fact that he cared deeply about political matters.[5] His message was intended, in part, to awaken his hearers to the importance of having men of virtue and competence at the helm of the state. Edwards declared, "Almost all the prosperity of a public society and civil community does under God depend on their rulers." He further stated, "The prosperity of a people depends more on their rulers than is commonly imagined." He went on to list the specific benefits that come to the public from gifted rulers. "Their influence has a tendency to promote their wealth." They "promote virtue amongst them." They even "promote their spiritual and eternal happiness." It is no wonder that Edwards affirmed that "such rulers" are "great gifts of the Most High to a people, and blessed tokens of his favor, and vehicles of his goodness to them, and therein images of his own Son, the grand medium of all God's goodness to fallen mankind."[6]

The Thinking of Jonathan Edwards Jr.

Edwards Jr. proclaimed that the prosperity and happiness of a political community (blessings which ultimately come from God) depend upon the presence of virtue in the social order, which in turn is contingent upon a faith commitment to the Lord as God.[7] In his sermon "The Necessity of the Belief of Christianity," Edwards used Psalm 144:15 as his text: "Yea, happy is that people whose GOD is the Lord." What exactly does this mean to say that Jehovah is the God of a particular people? Edwards affirmed, "The answer is when they believe, worship and obey the Lord or Jehovah, as the only true God, and that according to his revealed will."[8]

We must have, Edwards argued, "a full belief of the universal divine providence, of the accountableness of all men to God for all their conduct, and of a future equal retribution." "Some belief of a future state is necessary to our political prosperity." "Christianity is most excellently adapted to the ends of restraining men from vice and promoting that general practice of strict morality, which is so essential to the political prosperity of any people."[9]

The people who believe and worship Jehovah, maintained Edwards, have a benediction pronounced upon them. Appealing to his text, Edwards set forth a major argument in his sermon: "If we do so, the text pronounces us happy; and it plainly implies, that we cannot be happy on any condition short of this."[10]

Religion per se is not enough according to Edwards. The history of pagan religions proves the point. The gods embraced in the pagan world of the Greeks and Romans did not have holiness and righteousness. "All" of them "on many occasions" were characterized by "acting a most wicked part and indulging the most vilest lusts." They are remembered for the depth of their depravity—"their animosities and contentions" and "their intrigues and lusts."[11] Deities known for their iniquity resulted in societies overrun by vice: "All these ideas and practices tended to a general depravity of morals; so their efforts abundantly appeared in the vicious lives of the heathen world."[12]

The ancient world was known, affirmed Edwards, for the absence of "temperance, chastity, truth, justice and humanity."[13] He elaborated here on the absence of compassion in dominions under pagan gods—reminding his hearers of war, enslavement, assassinations, infanticide, the exhibition of gladiators, and suicide.[14] The evidence of history, Edwards contended, established his case that the only people who are happy are those whose God is the Lord. Edwards thus argued that whenever Americans believed and complied with the gospel, they were blessed with happiness.

The Beliefs of James Henley Thornwell

Thornwell believed that God in his providence establishes particular governments in the ongoing flow of history. "It is under Him," he affirmed, "that conventions are called, constitutions are framed and governments are erected.[15] Great political leaders, likewise, come from God himself. "They arise at His bidding, and execute His behests."[16] When Thornwell contemplated the great statesmen of world history, he thought of "the Father of the Country," George Washington.[17] He declared, "Moses and Joshua, Solon and Lycurgus, the Prince of Orange and Washington, were anointed and commissioned of heaven for the work they so happily performed."[18]

Thornwell believed that America was special. "There must be a grand imperial Republic on this continent," he contended, "and God will bring it about, and accomplish great purposes through it."[19] He embraced a redeemer-nation concept of the role that America was to play in world history.[20] "It was ours," he said, "to redeem the continent, to spread freedom, civilization and religion through the whole length of the land." He added, "We were a city set upon a hill, whose light was intended to shine upon every people and every land."[21]

Thornwell's love of the Union is seen in his call for repentance lest the chastening hand of divine providence fall upon America. "Sin," he said, "has been the ruin of every Empire that ever flourished and fell." Referring to the empires of Daniel's prophecy, he added, "Assyria,

Persia, Greece and Rome paid the penalties of the Divine law." Every government, like every individual, has but two choices: "The only alternative with States, as with their subjects, is, repent or perish."[22]

The necessity of repentance had been a long-standing concern in Thornwell's thinking. Commenting upon the death of Zachary Taylor in July 9, 1850, Thornwell wrote, "I suppose you have seen the account of the death of the President of the United States. What it means, it is difficult to conjecture. But it seems God is giving us warning after warning, line upon line, and precept upon precept." "Every good man," he said, "should be found constantly wrestling at the throne of grace for our bleeding and distracted country." He concluded, "I am satisfied that nothing but repentance on our part, and wonderful mercy on the part of God, can save us from the just consequences of our national sins."[23]

Thornwell was especially concerned about the moral behavior of America's politicians. He was saddened by the bitter railing and the use of weapons of personal abuse in the public arena.[24] He lamented inappropriate political discourse, "Instead of the language of calm deliberation, the representatives of the people have vied with each other in vituperation and abuse."[25]

Ultimately, to use Thornwell's imagery, the country passed over the brink into revolution. In his providentialist perspective, the dissolution and the war that followed were the display of God's "fierce anger" for the sins of the nation. It was lamented, and he sought to avert all of it in his preaching of repentance.[26]

The Perspectives of Robert Lewis Dabney

Dabney, like Thornwell, believed that America was special, embracing a redeemer-nation conception for the role that America was to play upon the world stage. He saw the light of America shining upon the darkness of the nations, teaching them to live in peace: "We hoped the Empire Republic would teach the angry nations nobler triumphs than those of war." He then expressed his vision for the role of America in these words: "That dream we had indulged" was "that here a nation was to grow up" which "should come by the righteous arts of peace to a greatness such as at last to shame and frighten war away from the family of kingdoms."[27]

Dabney taught that governments are raised by God under his providential superintendence.[28] This includes the appointment of specific statesmen. He described it not only as "God's ordinance," but also "if it be just, one of his greatest temporal blessings."[29] Political leaders are the very ministers of God, and they "rule by His providence."[30] Dabney illustrated his point by appealing to specific historical figures. He was impressed with William of Orange, describing him as "the Washington of the Netherlands, the most cool, deliberate, astute, far-seeing of statesmen, and most holy patriot and Christian."[31] He was enthused by his fellow Virginian, Thomas Jefferson, referring to him as "the sagacious Jefferson."[32]

Dabney did not insist upon theological orthodoxy as a requirement of political trust.[33] He did, however, insist upon a moral life: "Orthodoxy or spirituality are not qualifications requisite for its magistrates, according to the law of nature, but only secular virtue and intelligence."[34] He emphasized that political rulers must conduct themselves morally. He admonished, "The Christians of this country must sternly claim, that wicked men shall no longer hold the helm of state."[35] "Political orthodoxy," he said, "shall no longer atone for that worst offence against citizenship, a wicked life."[36] He clearly wanted an aristocracy of virtue.

Dabney embraced a Puritan kind of republicanism—a position that recognized the inevitable collapse of civilizations and the awareness that repentance or moral change is the answer to the demise of a society.[37] In the period preceding the Civil War, Dabney believed that the death of the American republic was imminent. He expressed his apprehension regarding the future of the nation. "A long farewell to that dream we had indulged," he asserted, "that here a nation was to grow up...composed of the strong, the free, the bold." "Our future," he lamented, "will be swallowed up by the devouring maw of strife."[38]

The Civil War did come to America in the providence of God. The divine chastisement, Dabney believed, was because of sin.[39] The Southern state governments, he contended, had failed in their judicial function, specifically with reference to their failure to prosecute duelists. He leveled this charge: "You have allowed too often the man of violence, the duelist…to stalk through the land with wrongs upon his angry tongue and blood upon his hand, while his crime was winked at by justice."[40]

The "peculiar sin" of the South, Dabney affirmed, was this "passion for bloody retaliation."[41] There indeed was a Southern "compulsion to avenge insult" on the dueling field.[42] The failure of the states to bring duelists to justice may have been due to the general climate of acceptance throughout the South of the right to defend one's honor. There was no need for the man who "killed his adversary in a personal quarrel" to "fear public disgrace."[43] Dabney opposed Southern thinking on this issue. He denounced his culture observing that the duelist with "blood upon his hand" had been "almost applauded by a corrupt public opinion."[44]

The propensity for embittered foes to meet on the dueling field is seen in a feud between Lincoln and the Illinois state auditor James Shields who challenged Lincoln to a duel in 1842 after Lincoln had ridiculed him. The two men met on Bloody Island in the Mississippi River near Saint Louis. The duel was averted, and the two men called a truce. Several weeks after the aborted duel, Lincoln informed an Illinois lawyer named Usher Linder, "I did not want to kill Shields and felt sure that I could disarm him, having had about a month to learn the broadsword exercise; and furthermore, I didn't want the damned fellow to kill me, which I rather think he would have done if we had selected pistols."[45] Lincoln ever remained ashamed about the incident and did not want to talk about it. Years later, he addressed a hotheaded officer: "Quarrel not at all. No man resolved to make the most of himself can spare time for personal contention."[46]

The doctrine of the divine superintendence of all events in history and politics was powerfully expounded by Edwards and his son

Jonathan in the North, and by Thornwell and Dabney in the South. Our consideration of the thought of Lincoln along with the teaching of his pastor, Phineas Gurley, appears in the next chapter. They too had a strong commitment to the Bible's teaching on the providence of God, and both men eloquently declared what they believed.

6

Lincoln and Phineas Gurley on the Mystery of Providence

New England Congregationalism and Southern Presbyterianism are not the only sources in American theology on the biblical doctrine of providence. We are able to find instruction in the meditations of an American president who mirrored the reflections of his pastor, Phineas Gurley. This is a remarkable thing when we remember the infidelity that Abraham Lincoln had displayed as a young man in his twenties after he left home and settled in New Salem, Illinois. It was an unbelief rooted in his self-sufficiency based upon his superior mind and personal virtue.

Lincoln's Moral and Intellectual Prominence

There was a stature and magnetism about Lincoln even while he was quite young. Men were willing to follow his leadership already in 1832 in the Black Hawk War when he was elected militia captain. Lincoln was idolized by his men. John M. Rutledge stated, "A better man I think never lived on the earth."[1] Admiration for him was rooted in his moral character. His goodness as a boy and a man was remarkable.[2] This is not to suggest that Lincoln's contemporaries were naïve concerning human nature. His legal associate Leonard Swett wrote, "There's a skeleton in Every house." At the same time, he advised William Herndon, "If Lincoln had some faults Washington had more—few men have less."[3] His stepmother, Sarah Bush Lincoln, testified, "Abe never gave me a cross word or look and never refused in fact, or Even in appearance, to do any thing I requested him." "He never told me a lie in his life." She summarized, "Abe was the best boy I Ever Saw or Ever Expect to see."[4]

Lincoln went out of his way to help creatures in distress.[5] His dear friend Joshua Speed relates the occasion when he and Lincoln along with their fellow lawyers in 1839 were returning to Springfield.[6] Lincoln was delayed along the way because "he had caught two little birds in his hand, which the wind had blown from their nest." Lincoln began to hunt for their nest and after finding it returned the birds to it. When Lincoln caught up with the party, "they laughed at him." "Said he, earnestly, 'I could not have slept tonight if I had not given those two little birds to their mother.'"[7]

His kind heart was accompanied with a powerful intellect, particularly reflected in the density of his writing and the absence of superfluity.[8] "He was not afraid of leaving things out because he disliked prolixity."[9] Leonard Swett for many years traveled the Eighth Judicial Circuit in Illinois with Lincoln. He wrote about "his purity of character and exalted morality."[10] But there was more to him than a nobility of character. Swett affirmed, "The great secret of his power as an orator, in my judgment, lay in the clearness and perspicuity of his statements." The same thing was demonstrated in the courtroom. Swett observed, "The first impression he generally conveyed was, that he had studied the case of his adversary better and more forcibly than his opponent could state it himself."[11] Judge David Davis worked with Lincoln for over ten years on the Eighth Judicial Circuit. He had a similar assessment and declared, "Mr. Lincoln had unsurpassed reasoning powers."[12]

Lawyers were not the only ones who were impressed with Lincoln. General William Tecumseh Sherman wrote, "Of all the men I have ever met, he seemed to possess more of the elements of greatness, combined with goodness, than any other."[13] After Pennsylvania Republican A. K. McClure visited the president-elect in Springfield in January 1861, he later affirmed, "Before half an hour had passed I learned not only to respect, but, indeed, to reverence the man."[14] A congressman from Illinois stated that people "felt the spell of Lincoln's voice and presence." A man from Wisconsin heard his voice, "which seemed to thrill every fiber of one's being." A woman who met Lincoln in the White House spoke about the "grandeur" of "the atmosphere" that surrounded him. An Illinois railroad conductor affirmed that "there was something about him which we plain people couldn't explain that made us stand a little in awe of him."[15]

Lincoln was different from those around him. Herndon, his legal partner from 1844 until Lincoln became president, wrote about his "intellectual superiority over other men" and the "grandeur of his character."[16] His mind according to Nathaniel Grigsby, his childhood friend, "soared above us."[17] Joshua Speed said, "His mind was a wonder to me." "Intense thought with him was the rule and not as with most of us the exception."[18]

Lincoln's Perception of the Divine

Young Lincoln's gifted mind moved in the direction of unbelief. This is not to say that he espoused atheism. He felt the presence of God in nature and knew that he would answer to the Almighty. On one occasion he shared his experience as a boy with Henry C. Whitney with whom he practiced law on the Eighth Judicial Circuit. Said Lincoln, "I used to wander out in the woods all by myself. It had a fascination for me which had an element of fear in it." "I knew that I was not alone just as well as I know that you are here now. Still I could see nothing and no one."[19] Lincoln likewise could not disown a deep sense of his moral accountability to God for his actions. He believed that we live in a moral universe and that a day of judgment is coming. During the Black Hawk War of 1832, an old Indian wandered into the camp of which Lincoln was captain. Lincoln's men would have killed him if Lincoln had not intervened stating, "We must not shed his blood. It must not be on our shirts."[20]

Unbelief and a Life without Hope

Lincoln sensed the presence of God in nature, and he knew that he would give an account to him of his life. Religious skepticism, nevertheless, dominated his mind during his six years in New Salem, a village of around one hundred people.[21] He imbibed the rationalism of Thomas Paine and saw fit to deny the divinity of Scripture and to attack biblical supernaturalism.[22] He wrote an essay against Christianity denying biblical inspiration and the divinity of Christ.[23] Samuel Hill, a kind neighbor, spared Lincoln's political future by tearing it out of his hand and throwing the manuscript into the stove.[24] Peter Cartwright, a Methodist evangelist, came to New Salem and preached the gospel in revival meetings.[25] Lincoln remained unmoved.[26] On one occasion, a neighbor lady, Parthena Hill, asked Lincoln whether he believed in a future state after death. Lincoln in unbelief answered, "I'm afraid there isn't. It isn't a pleasant thought to think that when we die that is the last of us."[27]

His unbelief may be the explanation for the waves of overwhelming sorrow that buried him in grief following the death of Ann Rutledge at the age of twenty-two.[28] Lincoln met her during his time in New Salem and fell deeply in love with her.[29] Herndon knew Ann personally and described her as "a beautiful girl," "the most popular young lady in the village." Lincoln's lifelong friend, William Greene, stated, "This young lady was a woman of Exquisite beauty, but her intellect was quick—Sharp—deep & philosophic as well as brilliant." "So sweet & angelic was she."[30] Lincoln, wrote Herndon, "whispered into her ear the old, old story. Her heart throbbed and her soul was thrilled with a joy as old the world itself."[31] "She consented to have Lincoln."[32] They were soon engaged. What they both desired, though, was not to be. The love of his life was struck with a fever and passed away on August 25, 1835.[33] Lincoln fell into "great mental depression" and "the deepest distress." He "wandered up and down the river and into the woods woefully abstracted." Lincoln shared with a friend his "indescribable grief" at the thought "that the snows and rains fall upon her grave." Some of his friends thought that he was on the borderline between sanity and insanity. He was found rambling in the woods and mumbling unintelligible words.[34] They sent him to live for a few weeks at the home of Bowling Green, the local justice of the peace, who lived a mile south of New Salem.[35] He cared for Lincoln and "gradually brought him back to reason."[36]

Becoming a New Man in Springfield

Lincoln at age twenty-two had arrived in New Salem in July 1831. Six years later, he moved twenty miles to Springfield. He rode a borrowed horse into the town of fifteen hundred inhabitants and carried all his personal belongings in two saddlebags.[37] He took his infidelity with him. In Springfield he would come into the office of the country clerk carrying a Bible. He would then read a chapter and proceed to argue against it.[38]

John Todd Stuart had a similar testimony. He had graduated from Centre College in Danville, Kentucky. His father, Robert Stuart, was a Presbyterian minister, the pastor at Walnut Hill Church in Lexington and professor of languages at Transylvania College. Stuart had moved to Springfield and opened a law practice. He encouraged Lincoln to study law and guided him in the study of books such as Sir William Blackstone's *Commentaries on the Laws of England*.[39] He eventually invited Lincoln to join him as a partner.[40] Stuart declared of Lincoln, "He was an avowed and open infidel." "He sometimes bordered on atheism." He "went further against Christian beliefs and doctrines and principles than any man I ever heard; he shocked me."[41]

Transformation, nevertheless, was going to come. Stuart lived to see the day when Lincoln had thrown off his infidelity. Stuart told Lincoln in the course of the Civil War that neither he nor "any other man can make it go on just as" they wished. "*I believe that Providence is carrying on this thing*," Stuart declared. Lincoln then responded with great emphasis, "Stuart that is just my opinion."[42] Another friend named Orville Browning declared, "I do know that he was not a scoffer at religion. During our long and intimate acquaintance and intercourse, I have no recollection of ever having heard an irreverent word fall from his lips."[43] More than that, Browning stated, "He was always naturally a very religious man."[44]

Lincoln clearly did not remain what he had been. As the years passed, Lincoln came to understand that "the incomprehensible might still be true."[45] Further suffering intervened effecting change within.[46] Years later, Lincoln wrote a letter comforting a young girl whose father had been killed in the Civil War. "In this sad world of ours," he affirmed, "sorrow comes to all." "I have had experience to know what I say."[47] Herndon notes, "He was a sad-looking man; his melancholy dripped from him as he walked."[48] The trials and sorrows of life, though, eventually extracted the rationalism that had imbedded itself within him. We see indications of this during his time as a lawyer in Springfield, Illinois, and then again as president of the United States in Washington, DC.

His son Eddie Lincoln died in 1850 at the age of three and a half.[49] Lincoln did not respond in an atheistic manner rejecting the pastoral ministry of Reverend James Smith, a native of Glasgow, Scotland.[50] Smith had transitioned from an affinity with New School Presbyterianism into the camp of Old School Presbyterianism in the 1840s.[51] Lincoln and his wife Mary Todd looked to the new minister at the First Presbyterian Church in Springfield for pastoral comfort in their time of grief.[52] After the funeral the Lincolns began to rent a pew in the church. In the late 1850s, Lincoln started to become more of a regular attendee, while his wife appeared before the session and having given her testimony was received into the membership.[53] The minister regularly visited the Lincoln home at the intersection of Eighth and Jackson, and Lincoln gave careful attention to Smith's theological work *The Christian's Defense*.[54] He maintained that the book "had led him to change his views about the Christian religion."[55]

By January 1851 Lincoln had abandoned his earlier skepticism regarding the existence of the soul after death.[56] He gave a remarkable message to his father conveyed by those who had notified him that his father would soon pass away.[57] "Tell him to remember to call upon and confide in our great and good and merciful Maker, who will not turn away from him in any extremity," Lincoln said. "He notes the fall of a sparrow, and numbers the hairs of our heads; and He will not forget the dying man who puts his trust in him." "If it be his lot to go now he will soon have a joyous meeting with the many loved ones gone before, and where the rest of us, through the help of God, hope ere long to join them."[58]

A Deepening Faith in the Nation's Capital

The same faith regarding the afterlife came through during his time as president. Joshua Speed wrote, "After he was elected President, he sought to become a believer."[59] We see something of this in his response to the death of his son Willie on February 20, 1862.[60] He said, "My poor boy, he was too good for this earth. God has called him home." He then raised his thoughts upward declaring, "I know that he is much better off in heaven, but then we loved him so."[61] There is also the testimony of Joshua Speed who visited him at the White House shortly prior to his Second Inaugural. Speed witnessed the words spoken by an older lady: "Good-bye, Mr. Lincoln." "I shall probably never see you again till we meet in heaven." The president responded, "That you wish me to get there is, I believe, the best wish you could make for me. Good-bye."[62] The position that Lincoln held regarding heaven was later mirrored in the effort of twelve-year-old Tad Lincoln to comfort his mother after the assassination of his father. He likewise expressed his own faith saying, "Papa was good and he is gone to heaven. He is happy there. He is with God and brother Willie."[63]

We find a humble and teachable spirit in Lincoln in his years as president under the ministry of Reverend Phineas Gurley, the pastor at New York Avenue Presbyterian Church in Washington, DC.[64] Gurley had graduated first in his class at Princeton Theological Seminary in 1840, studying under the renowned theologians Archibald Alexander and Charles Hodge.[65] Gurley was a mainstream Reformed theologian, a very different preacher than the hyper-Calvinist Baptist pastors who ministered to his father and mother when Lincoln was growing up. Lincoln loved to hear Gurley preach and regularly attended upon his ministry.[66]

It was Gurley who preached the funeral sermon in the East Room of the White House for Willie Lincoln who died on February 20, 1862, at the age of eleven.[67] Gurley endeavored to present what he called "a clear and scriptural view of the providence of God." He noted that providence can appear as "a mysterious dealing" and encouraged the Lincolns to "acknowledge" the "hand" of God and to "hear His voice, and inquire after His will."[68] A year and half later, Lincoln heard Gurley expound Proverbs 16:9 at New York Avenue Presbyterian Church: "A man's heart deviseth his way; but the Lord directs his steps." Gurley drew attention to the fact that man is a free moral agent. But there is more to it than that. He added, "It is also true that God governs the world."[69]

Lincoln's Fundamental Belief

Gurley's biblical teaching resonated with Lincoln. His friend Orville Browning declared that he knew that "Lincoln" was "a firm believer in a superintending and overruling Providence, and in super-natural agencies and events."[70] This is not to say that Lincoln embraced the pagan idea of fatalism. This is a mischaracterization that historians commonly make.[71] The biblical doctrine of providence is very different from fatalism. The Bible presents a personal God who answers prayer.[72] Reverend Byron Sutherland, the pastor of First Presbyterian Church in Washington for forty-five years, heard Lincoln speak about God and the war in 1862. Said the president, "I am not fatalist. I believe" that "men are responsible beings." "God" will "hold them, to a strict personal account for the deeds done in the body."[73]

Lincoln's views on the will of God and providence coincided with the Westminster Confession of Faith. The Westminster divines, for example, asserted, "God, from all eternity, did by the most wise and holy counsel of his own will, freely, and unchangeably ordain whatsoever comes to pass" (iii.i). They further stated that God does "direct…all…things, from the greatest even to the least, by his most wise and holy providence" (v.i). Lincoln embraced these perspectives. After he was assassinated, John Hay, one of Lincoln's secretaries, found a private meditation that Lincoln had written on the divine will. Lincoln was reflecting on the presence of God in the Civil War.[74] He wrote, "The will of God prevails." "I am almost ready to say that this is probably true—that God wills this contest, and wills that it shall not end yet."[75]

Lincoln had affirmed the same line of thinking in a letter to the editor of the *Frankfort Commonwealth*, dated April 4, 1864. Reflecting upon the Civil War that had engulfed the nation, Lincoln wrote, "I claim not to have controlled events, but confess plainly that events have controlled me." God was the one who was controlling events and manifesting his justice for the "complicity" of both North and South in a "great wrong."

The Westminster Confession had maintained the divine use of secondary causes in effecting his will, while maintaining the freedom of God to work directly in history apart from human agency: "God, in his ordinary providence, maketh use of means, yet is free to work without, above, and against them, at his pleasure" (v.iii). Lincoln embraced the same position. It is not correct to say that Lincoln had a "fundamental conviction" that men and women do not have a free will.[76] If that were the case, human beings could not be held accountable for their actions. Lincoln, though, did believe in personal responsibility and divine justice. Lincoln stood with Gurley who believed that man is rational and free, "an accountable moral agent."[77] His private contemplation on the divine will asserted, "The human instrumentalities, working just as they do, are of the best adaptation to effect his purpose." God, though, could have effected his purposes directly, "By his mere great power, on the minds of the now contestants, He could have either *saved* or *destroyed* the Union without a human contest."[78]

The Westminster divines had drawn attention to mystery in the unfolding of the divine will in history. The "unsearchable wisdom" of God is reflected in "his providence" (v.iv). Lincoln came to the same fundamental conception about God.[79] His ways are past finding out![80] He mused in private, "In the present civil war it is quite possible that God's purpose is something different from the purpose of either party."[81] He publicly declared the same thought in his greatest speech, the Second Inaugural Address.[82] He distinguished between the purposes of the North and South and the purpose of God: "Both read the same Bible, and prayed to the same God; and each invokes his aid against the other." "The purposes of both could not be answered—that of neither has been answered fully. The Almighty has his own purpose."[83]

7

The Hand of God in the Life of Lincoln

A Man from the Backwoods

We have considered Lincoln's thought on the mystery of providence. What did he believe about divine providence in relationship to his own life? On August 22, 1864, Lincoln spoke to the 166th Ohio Regiment in Washington, DC, who were on their way home. In his short speech, he expressed amazement at the course of his life.[1] Said Lincoln, "I happen temporarily to occupy this big White House. I am a living witness that any one of your children may look to come here as my father's child has."[2] Herndon also marveled at Lincoln's life story. "It will always be a wonder," he said, that "from such restricted and unpromising opportunities in early life, Mr. Lincoln grew into the great man he was."[3] Lincoln himself "condensed" his "early life" into "a single sentence"—"The short and simple annals of the poor."[4] "I have seen a great deal of the backside of this world," he said.[5]

Lincoln was born on February 12, 1809, on Sinking Spring Farm in a sixteen-by-eighteen-foot log cabin with a dirt floor eighteen miles southeast of Elizabethtown, Kentucky.[6] When he was two years old, he moved with his father Thomas, his mother Nancy, and his older sister Sarah fourteen miles northeast to another farm on Knob Creek.[7] At the age of seven, he moved with his family to the Pigeon Creek, a settlement of about twenty cabins in southern Indiana, a mile and a half east of the village of Gentryville.[8] Unlike Kentucky, Indiana provided secure land titles under the Northwest Ordinance. "The Country was a wilderness." When Lincoln's father "landed in Indiana," he had to "cut his way to his farm with the Axe felling the forest as he went."[9] It was a "scantily settled region" with rolling hills and dense woods, abounding with wolves, panthers, wild cats, and bears.[10]

The family having settled in Indiana initially lived in a small structure enclosed on three sides with a roaring fire for protection on the fourth side.[11] At last, they moved into an eighteen-by-twenty-foot cabin of "hewed logs," which had a loft where Abraham slept.[12] When Lincoln's stepmother arrived, "there was no floor or Door to the House of her Husband, no furniture of any Kind, no Beds or Bedding." She "at once had floor Laid in the House, Doors & Windows put in."[13] It was an isolated area to live in with maybe one family to every four square miles.[14] Life was hard, and Lincoln received little education: "All his school days, added together would not make a year in the aggregate."[15]

Lincoln turned twenty-one, and it was time to move again. Illinois would be the final home of his father, Thomas Lincoln.[16] Abraham helped with the move from the thick forests of southern Indiana to the unplowed prairie grasses of Illinois where he helped his father build a log cabin ten miles west of Decatur on the north side of the Sangamon River.[17] Herndon reflected upon the scene: "As these humble emigrants entered the new State little did the curious people in the towns through which they passed dream that the obscure and penniless driver who yelled his commands to the oxen would yet become Chief Magistrate of the greatest nation of modern times."[18]

Exalted to the Heights

Lincoln became in the view of Herndon "the great American, the grand, central figure in American—perhaps the world's—history."[19] As president, notes Herndon, he "was surrounded by wealth, power, fashion, influence." Did his "exalted status" change him? "Lincoln had not changed a particle," Herndon answered.[20] For John Hay, assistant private secretary to the president, "Lincoln, with all his foibles" was "the greatest character since Christ."[21]

How did all of this come about? As Joshua Speed reflected upon Lincoln's "rise from point to point…until he reached the presidency," it all seemed "more like fiction than fact." He concluded, "None but a genius like his could have accomplished so much, and none but a government like ours could produce such a man." He used this imagery: "It gave the young eagle scope for his wing. He tried it and soared to the top!"[22] There was also an awareness that God was behind these events. Sojourner Truth, after having traveled from Michigan in the autumn of 1864, visited the president at the White House. She expressed to him her apprehensions, "Mr. President, when you first took your seat I feared you would be torn to pieces, for I likened you to Daniel, who was thrown into the lions' den; and if the lions did not tear you to pieces, I knew that it would be God that had saved you." She then shared with him her thinking regarding the Emancipation Proclamation in which Lincoln had freed the slaves in the states which had rebelled. "I thank God," she said, "that you were the instrument selected by him and the people to do it."[23]

John Hay believed that divine providence had placed Lincoln in the highest office in the land. He commented, "There is no man in the country, so wise, so gentle and so firm. I believe the hand of God placed him where he is."[24] Lincoln had made a similar statement when he eulogized the Kentucky statesman, Henry Clay, on July 6, 1852. Lincoln asked, "Our country is prosperous and powerful; but could it have been quite all it has been, and is, and is to be, without Henry Clay?" He answered, "Such a man the times have demanded, and such, in the providence of God was given to us." He then made a statement that Hay, no doubt, would have accepted as having a future fulfillment in Lincoln himself: "Let us strive to deserve, as far as mortals may, the continued care of Divine Providence, trusting that, in future national emergencies, He will not fail to provide us the instruments of safety and security."[25]

What perspective did Lincoln have concerning his own rise from obscurity to the heights of political power? He was actually amazed at the direction of his life. A Canadian editor named Josiah Blackburn interviewed the president and recorded this statement concerning his position in relationship to the Civil War: "It is very strange that I, a boy brought up in the woods, and seeing, as it were, but little of the world, should be drifted into the very apex of this great event."[26] Orville Browning provided insight into Lincoln's deepest conviction: "I know that he believed the destinies of men were, or, at least, that his own destiny was, shaped, and controlled, by an intelligence and power higher and greater than his own, and which he could neither control nor thwart."[27]

Browning's assessment of what Lincoln believed about himself matches the testimony of Reverend Noyes W. Miner, a Baptist minister and neighbor friend of Lincoln in Springfield. Miner visited the White House in April 1862 and related the president's comments regarding the burdens of the office which he held. Said Lincoln, "I would gladly, if I could, take my neck from under the yoke and go home with you to Springfield and live, as I used, in peace with my friends, than to endure this harassing kind of life." Then Lincoln added, "But it has pleased Almighty God to place me in my present position, and, looking up to Him for wisdom and divine guidance, I must work out my destiny as best I can."[28]

These perspectives had deep roots in Christian political thought. In his Preface to his biblical commentary on the Psalms, Calvin asserted concerning King David that "he was taken from the sheepfold, and elevated to the rank of supreme authority."[29] Every political leader without exception, Calvin maintained, is put into place by God. It is due to the "providence of God" that the Lord appoints "what king he pleases."[30] In his commentary on Romans 13, Calvin contended that "they who rule" have "not ascended by their own power into this high station, but have been placed there by the Lord's hand."[31]

Reverend Phineas Gurley

We also need to remember the influence of Phineas Gurley when it comes to the president's faith commitment. Reverend Gurley was the pastor-theologian from Hamilton, New York. President Lincoln was the lawyer-politician from Springfield, Illinois. A man from the North and a man from the West, both summoned to the same place at the same time, the capital of an endangered nation.[32] It is noteworthy that Gurley was able to accept the call to be the pastor of New York Avenue Presbyterian Church because he had previously turned down an offer in 1860 to become professor of pastoral theology at Princeton Theological Seminary.[33]

Gurley was precisely the kind of man that Lincoln needed in a time of the greatest crisis. He was deeply intellectual, an orthodox Old School Presbyterian theologian, and a pastor who would faithfully care for the soul of the president.[34] He was there for the president in his times of need—at the death of Willie and at the bedside of the president as he lay dying from an assassin's bullet.[35] He was there for the broken family and delivered the president's funeral sermon on April 19, 1865, in the East Room of the White House. He continued to bring comfort, delivering the benediction, when Lincoln was laid to rest at the Oak Ridge Cemetery on May 4, 1865—a service which concluded with the singing of a hymn which Gurley had written.[36]

Lincoln's moral character was incorruptible. He had once exhorted potential lawyers, "Resolve to be honest at all events, and if in your judgment you cannot be an honest lawyer, resolve to be honest without being a lawyer."[37] Gurley recognized that Lincoln was not a hypocrite. In his funeral sermon for Lincoln, he said this concerning the man whom he had come to know over the preceding four years: "His integrity was thorough, all pervading, all controlling, and incorruptible."[38] "He rose to the dignity and momentousness of the occasion, saw his duty as the Chief Magistrate of a great and imperiled people, and he determined to do his duty, and his whole duty, seeking the guidance and leaning on the arm of Him of Whom it is written: 'He giveth to the faint, and to them who have no might he increaseth strength.'"[39] Gurley then concluded the funeral service by placing his hand on Lincoln's coffin and uttering a word of benediction in the presence of the six hundred people who attended, which included General Ulysses S. Grant dressed in full uniform: "You, our honored friend and head…will survive yourself and triumph over the injustice of time."[40]

Trusting in the Lord

Lincoln had explicitly referred to his own faith in his farewell speech given on February 11, 1861, at the railroad station in Springfield, Illinois, just before he boarded the train that would take him to Washington, DC. Lincoln declared to over a thousand people who had gathered to bid him farewell, "I now leave, not knowing when, or whether ever, I may return, with a task before me greater than that which rested upon Washington." He then referred to God: "Without the assistance of that Divine Being, who ever attended him, I cannot succeed. With that assistance I cannot fail. Trusting in Him, who can go with me, and remain with you and be every where for good, let us confidently hope that all will yet be well." He concluded by referring to prayer: "To His care commending you, as I hope in your prayers you will commend me. I bid you an affectionate farewell."[41]

He trusted in God. That is what Lincoln announced to the world. He called upon the nation to consider the advantage of doing the same in his First Inaugural delivered three weeks after his departure from Springfield: "Intelligence, patriotism, Christianity, and a firm reliance on Him who has never yet forsaken this favored land are still competent to adjust in the best way all our present difficulty."[42]

Lincoln, trapped in the mire of unbelief, was extricated, subdued, and brought to a teachable frame.[43] He was willing to sit at the feet of a man of God. "He held a pew in the [*New York Avenue*] Presbyterian Church" and "often attended service there."[44] He became a humble student of Scripture.[45] When his dear friend Joshua Speed visited

Lincoln at the Soldiers' Home three miles from the White House in the summer of 1864, he found him reading the Bible.[46] Speed confessed that he himself had not recovered from his skepticism.[47] The president according to Speed laid his hand on his shoulder and said, "You are wrong Speed, take all of this book upon reason that you can, and the balance on faith, and you will live and die a happier and better man."[48]

Lincoln affirmed that the Bible was "the best gift God has given to man."[49] His position was clearly stated: "All the good the Saviour gave to the world was communicated through this book. But for it we could not know right from wrong. All things most desirable for man's welfare, here and hereafter, are to be portrayed in it."[50]

This perspective on the Bible explains why Lincoln on a steamboat trip down to Norfolk "disappeared" and was found sitting "in an out of the way place" and "reading a dog eared *pocket* copy of the New Testament all by himself."[51] We find the same thing in the testimony of Orville Browning who maintained that he would "not infrequently" accompany the president and Mrs. Lincoln to the New York Avenue Presbyterian Church. "Sometimes, after services were over," said Browning, "I would return with them to the White House to dinner and spend the afternoon with him in the Library. On such occasions I have seen him reading the Bible."[52]

Nancy Hanks Lincoln

How did these changes come about? How could it be that Leonard Swett could say of Lincoln that "his whole life was a life of love to God, and love of his neighbor as of himself"?[53] Was this the answer of God to the prayers of Nancy Hanks Lincoln, the mother of the president?

She was a remarkable woman. Dennis Hanks, her first cousin, describes her as "one of the very best women in the whole race, known for kindness—tenderness—charity & love to the world."[54] She was "highly intellectual by nature, had a strong memory, acute judgment, and was cool and heroic."[55] Nathaniel Grigsby who went to school with Lincoln asserted, "She was a brilliant woman."[56] Herndon wrote about a conversation that he once had with his law partner, Lincoln: "It was about 1850, when he and I were driving in his one-horse buggy to the court in Menard county, Illinois." "As the buggy jolted over the road, he added ruefully, 'God bless my mother; all that I am or ever hope to be I owe to her.'" "He was sad and absorbed."[57]

Lincoln's mother had often read to her children from the Bible.[58] But Lincoln lost her when he was only nine years of age of "milk sick," a disease contracted from drinking the milk of cows that had grazed on the poisonous white snakeroot. Herndon provided the farewell scene: "The mother knew she was going to die, and called the children to her bedside. She was very weak, and the children leaned over while she gave her last message. Placing her feeble hand on little Abe's head she told him to be kind and good to his father and sister; to both she said, 'Be good to one another,' expressing a hope that they might live, as they had been taught by her, to love their kindred and worship God."[59]

This was the parting counsel of his mother, described by Nathaniel Grigsby as "a Christian woman of the Baptist per swasion."[60] These were words that Lincoln could never forget. He helped his father build his mother's coffin, and he was the one who wrote a letter to Pastor David Elkins, a pioneer circuit preacher, requesting that he travel to perform a funeral service for his mother—which he eventually did, preaching at her grave.[61] He referred to her as "my angel mother."[62] This was an apt designation for a woman who lived with "thoughts of Him who watched over them by night and day."[63]

Herndon drew attention to the place that lowly, forgotten saints have in the plan of God: "Amid the miserable surroundings of a home in the wilderness Nancy Hanks passed across the dark river. Though of lowly birth, the victim of poverty, and hard usage, she takes a place in history as the mother of a son who liberated a race of men."[64]

Freedom Brought by Father Abraham

On August 22, 1862, Lincoln had written, "My paramount object in this struggle *is* to save the Union, and is *not* to save or to destroy slavery."[65] Lincoln initially announced this position due to the fact that he needed to keep the border states in the Union.[66] He modified his policy by the summer of 1864. The peace terms that he articulated included the nonnegotiable necessity of "the abandonment of slavery." He pointed out that the more than 100,000 black soldiers in the Union army at that time were fighting for "the promise of freedom." He said, "The promise being made, must be kept."[67] In accordance with this determination, Lincoln insisted that the passage of the Thirteenth Amendment be part of the Republican Party platform for the 1864 presidential election.[68] The platform committed the Republicans to the "utter and complete extirpation" of slavery "from the soil of the Republic" and to "an amendment to the Constitution" which "shall terminate and forever prohibit the existence of Slavery within the limits of the jurisdiction of the United States."[69]

He kept his promise and would not budge from his determination to put an end to slavery. He thereby earned the everlasting gratitude of the newly emancipated slaves. On April 4, 1865, Lincoln walked the streets of Richmond, the Confederate capital, which had been evacuated two days earlier. Thousands of newly freed black slaves came out to see him. They danced around him in an "uncontrollable ecstasy of delight."[70] One woman called out, "I know that I am free for I have seen father Abraham and felt him." One man knelt before the president and Lincoln responded, "You must kneel to God only and thank him for the liberty you will hereafter enjoy."[71]

8

The Work That God Had Done

A Foreboding Sense of Doom

Lincoln's mother passed away from this world on October 5, 1818. Just over a year later, his father Thomas Lincoln married Sarah Bush Johnston who welcomed the two Lincoln orphans, twelve-year-old Sarah and her brother ten-year-old Abraham, into her affections.[1] On January 31 and February 1, 1861, Lincoln bade farewell to his stepmother before he left for the White House.[2] A foreboding had already captured her heart. Herndon visited her in September 1865, five months after the assassination. Herndon wrote, "She broke down and wept bitterly." "I did not want Abraham to run for President," she sobbed, "and did not want to see him elected. I was afraid something would happen to him, and when he came to see me, after he was elected President. I still felt, and my heart told me, that something would befall Abe, and that I should never see him again."[3]

Lincoln, too, had a sense that something dreadful was going to happen to him.[4] In early April 1865, the president had a haunting dream about himself in which he heard sobbing in the White House. As he entered the East Room he came upon mourners surrounding a corpse whose face was covered. He asked one of the soldiers on guard, "Who is dead in the White House?" "'The President,' was his answer; 'he was killed by an assassin.'"[5] At the last cabinet meeting that Lincoln held on April 14, 1865, the very day that he was assassinated, he remarked about "a peculiar dream of the previous night" in which he was "floating on some vast and indistinct expanse toward an unknown shore." He commented that whenever he had had the same dream in the past it "had been followed by some important event or disaster."[6]

Mercy for the Rebels

The long bloodbath of the Civil War was finally coming to an end, but Lincoln's premonition would soon come to pass at the hand of John Wilkes Booth. Robert E. Lee had just surrendered the Army of Northern Virginia to Ulysses S. Grant at Appomattox on April 9, 1865. Neither Lee nor his soldiers were sent to a prisoner-of-war camp.[7] They were released on parole. Grant promised that there would be no reprisals and no trials for treason. Union troops had suffered over half a million casualties at the hands of rebel troops.[8] Yet Grant fed Lee's hungry soldiers who were then allowed to go home with their horses for spring plowing.[9]

Grant extended mercy in accordance with Lincoln's desires which the president had made known in a meeting on March 28, 1865. Lincoln had expressed that he wanted to extend "the most liberal and honorable terms." Mercy for the defeated Confederates was what he wanted: "Let them all go, officers and all. I want submission and no more bloodshed. Let them have their horses to plow with, and, if you like, their guns to shoot crows with. I want no one punished."[10] Lincoln in all of this presented a strong contrast to the feelings of others in the North. A Reverend Mr. Black, for example, declared, "Let Davis and Beauregard be captured, to meet the same fate as Haman. Hang them up on Mason's and Dixon's line, that traitors may be warned."[11]

The wishes that the president shared with Grant had been articulated on other occasions as well. When Lincoln toured Richmond on April 4, 1865, he exhorted General Godfrey Weitzel regarding his treatment of the conquered people. "Let 'em up easy," he said.[12] In a conversation with General Sherman during the conferences at City Point, March 27–28, 1865, Lincoln asserted that "he contemplated no revenge" and "no harsh measures" for the Confederate soldiers. He believed that the suffering that they had already endured in the war would make them "more submissive to law."[13]

With respect to the president of the Confederacy, Jefferson Davis, Lincoln rejected the position that he should be punished quoting the words of Jesus, "Judge not that ye be not judged."[14] More specifically, he suggested two possibilities for the defeated president. On one occasion near the end of the war, he said that "if he had his way, he would let him die in peace on his southern plantation."[15] At another time, he stated, "I hope he will mount a fleet horse, reach the shores of the Gulf of Mexico, and drive so far into the waters that we shall never see him again."[16]

An Actor Gripped by Rage

Booth was a madman who could not see reality for what it was. In his derangement, he could not see the spirit of clemency in Lincoln's heart.[17] He appears to have been oblivious, for example, to the severe punitive measures taken by Oliver Cromwell against the Royalist forces in the English Civil War. He, no doubt, was likewise ignorant of the fact that Martin Luther had advised the execution of seditious peasants who began their revolt in the Black Forest region of Germany on May 30, 1524. "A seditious person," wrote Luther, "is an outlaw before God and the emperor." Sedition in the view of Luther was a heinous crime which demanded swift justice. "Whoever is the first to put him to death does right and well," he contended. He reasoned, "For if a man is in open rebellion, everyone is both his judge and executioner."[18] God according to Luther is the one who avenges rebellion. He thundered, "The peasants have a bad conscience and an unjust cause, and that any peasant who is killed in body and soul is eternally the devil's." In defense of his position, Luther affirmed, "If anyone thinks this is too harsh, let him remember that rebellion is intolerable."[19]

A great rebellion had taken place in the United States. The rebels could well expect justice as the war concluded, but Lincoln had decided on a course of mercy. Booth, though, viewed events from the perspective of insanity. He lived in darkness, ignorant of the light of history. Having no knowledge, he called evil good, and good evil. Lincoln for him was a tyrant. Thus followed the tragedy on the evening of Good Friday, April 14, 1865. Booth slipped into the presidential box at Ford's Theatre, pulled out a derringer pistol, shot the president in the head, leaped on to the stage, and cried out *Sic semper tyrannis.* Lincoln slumped forward with a mortal wound and died at 7:22 a.m. the next morning.

Sad to say, there were Americans who expressed their sympathetic participation in the murder.[20] In Houston came the newspaper pronouncement: "From now until God's judgment day the minds of men will not cease to thrill at the killing of Abraham Lincoln."[21] The Dallas *Herald* declared, "God Almighty ordered this event."[22]

What Lincoln Had Long Understood

In the summer of 1864, the president had said, "I feel a presentiment that I shall not outlast the rebellion. When it is over, my work will be done."[23] He had said something similar to Harriet Beecher Stowe when she visited him at the White House in November 1862. Commenting on the Civil War, Lincoln told her, "Whichever way it ends, I have the impression that I shan't last long after it's over."[24] The president could never forget that he was in a dangerous position. He kept a southern newspaper clipping on his desk that offered $100,000 for his "miserable traitorous head."[25] It reflected the foreboding sentiment within him while serving as president, but he had a sense of things to come even earlier than this.

When Lincoln bade farewell to Herndon in their law office in Springfield, he even then had an intuitive sense that he would not be returning.[26] Herndon wrote, "He said the sorrow of parting from his old associations was deeper than most persons would imagine, but it was marked in his case because of the feeling which had become irrepressible that he would never return alive."[27] "He always contended that he was doomed to a sad fate, and he repeatedly said to me when we were alone in our office: 'I am sure I shall meet with some terrible end.'"[28]

Lincoln's premonition may have contributed to a sense within him that his doom was inevitable no matter what he did or did not do.[29] While conversing with Noah Brooks in the spring of 1863, Lincoln remarked, "I long ago made up my mind that if anybody wants to kill me, he will do it. If I wore a shirt of mail and kept myself surrounded by a bodyguard, it would be all the same."[30] He told his private secretary John Nicolay, "If anybody has the disposition to kill me he will find opportunity."[31] The president informed a White House employee named Thomas Pendel, "I do not like to be guarded, but I have received a number of threatening letters lately. I have no fears, however."[32] Herndon stated, "Mr. Lincoln for years had a presentiment that he would reach a high place and then be stricken down in some tragic way. He took no precaution to keep out of the way of danger."[33] We something of this on July 12, 1864, when Lincoln oblivious to his own safety stood on the parapet at Fort Stevens and came under fire from Confederate sharpshooters under the command of General Jubal Early. A soldier standing next to the president was struck dead by one of their bullets.[34] Whether or not it happened or not, legend has it that Oliver Wendell Holmes yelled out, "Get down, you damn fool!"

We find the same attitude of disregard for his own personal safety in a comment made on April 5, 1865, the day after the president visited the Confederate capital of Richmond, which had been evacuated three days earlier. Edward Ripley, a Union officer from Vermont, informed Lincoln that there was a plot against his life. The president replied, "It is impossible for me to adopt and follow your suggestions." He then made an unrealistic statement in light of the intense hatred that many had toward him: "I cannot bring myself to believe that any human being lives who would do me any harm."[35] He had made a similar statement to congressman James S. Rollins: "I don't see what on God's earth any man would wish to kill me for, for there is not a human being living to whom I would not extend a favor and make them happy if it was in my power to do so."[36] Even though someone had shot a bullet through Lincoln's hat one August night in 1864 as he was riding horseback to the Soldiers' Home in Washington, he disregarded the pleas of Edwin Stanton and Ward Hill Lamon not to go out the night in which he was assassinated.[37]

Lincoln had a premonition, an inward sense that his days would soon come to an end, but he lived with faith in the present and hope for the future. The evidence strongly indicates that he knew God as his Creator and Redeemer and fully trusted in him.

Lincoln and the Twofold Knowledge of God

Calvin in continuity with medieval theology wrote about the twofold knowledge of God. First, "the Lord shows himself to be simply the Creator. Then in the face of Christ he shows himself the Redeemer."[38] The knowledge of God as our Creator gives us to understand that "not only does he sustain this universe (as he once founded it) by his boundless might, regulate it by his wisdom, preserve it by his goodness, and especially rule mankind by his righteousness and judgment, bear with it in his mercy, watch over it by his protection: but also that no drop will be found either of wisdom and light, or of righteousness or power or rectitude, or of genuine truth, which does not flow from him."[39] It is the knowledge of God as Creator that creates piety, which is "reverence joined with love of God which the knowledge of his benefits induces."[40]

Piety is indispensable, but there is more that is necessary. We must come to know God as our Redeemer. Calvin stated, "Since we have fallen from life unto death, the whole knowledge of God the Creator that we have discussed would be useless unless faith also followed, setting forth for us God our Father in Christ."[41] "We must understand," insisted Calvin, "that as long as Christ remains outside of us, and we are separated from him, all that he has suffered and done for the salvation of the human race remains useless and of no value for us." We must have faith so that Christ is in us, and we are in him.[42] The good news is this: "When first even the least drop of faith is instilled in our minds, we begin to contemplate God's face, peaceful and calm and gracious toward us."[43]

Lincoln explicitly referred to the fact that God was his Creator, referring to "our great and good and merciful Maker."[44] But there are also indications that he knew God as his Redeemer. He told Newton Bateman who later became the president of Knox College in 1874: "I know that liberty is right, for Christ teaches it, and Christ is God."[45] He stated that he loved the preaching of Reverend Gurley because of its gospel content. "I like Gurley," said Lincoln. "He don't preach politics. I get enough of that through the week, and when I go to church, I like to hear the gospel."[46] This statement matches the testimony of John H. Wickizer, a legal colleague of Lincoln on the Eight Judicial Circuit, who said, "I think he believed in 'Jesus Christ, and him crucified.'"[47]

Leonard Swett indicated that Lincoln had "a feeling of religious reverence, a belief in God and his justice," a conviction of "the ultimate triumph of the right and the overthrow of the wrong."[48] Gurley in his funeral sermon for the president told of one occasion in the darkest days of the Civil War in which Lincoln had said the following to Gurley and a group of ministers who had gathered at the White House: "Gentlemen, my hope of success in this great and terrible struggle rests on that immutable foundation, the justice and goodness of God, and when events are very threatening and prospects very dark, I still hope in some way which man can not see all will be well in the end, because our cause is just, and God is on our side."[49]

Slavery and the Order of Nature

The question has been asked as to how it could be that the theologians of Lincoln's generation were "able to offer so little of theological profundity concerning the religious meaning of the Civil War?"[50] Charles Hodge at Princeton Theological Seminary is an exception at this point. He provided a profound theological interpretation. Hodge offered his reflections upon the Civil War, the assassination of the president, slavery, and divine providence in the July 1865 edition of the *Princeton Review.* He rehearsed themes that had long been acknowledged in disparate places—in the New England theology, Old School Presbyterianism, and the speeches of Abraham Lincoln. God, he wrote, "is everywhere present…controlling, guiding, and directing the action of second causes, so that all events occur according to the counsel of his will." At the same time, he "governs free agents with certainty, but without destroying their liberty."[51]

Hodge, no doubt, heard the reports regarding the inhumane treatment of slaves. A soldier in the 90th New York, for example, spoke about "this cursed slavery that gives one man power over another to whip or to do as he pleases with them."[52] Even Robert Dabney, a defender of the biblical legitimacy of slavery, acknowledged that the law often left slaves without legal protection. The slaveholders, he said, "must be willing to recognize and grant in slaves those rights which are a part of our essential humanity, some of which are left without recognition or guarantee by law, and some infringed by law." He agreed that "these are the rights of immortal and domestic beings."[53]

The absence of fundamental human rights for the slaves was highly problematic. There were Old School Presbyterians in the South who admitted that this was the case. An example of this is seen in Benjamin Warfield's maternal grandfather, Robert Breckinridge, a professor of theology at Danville Seminary in Kentucky. He attacked slavery as a "great evil" and promised to "rid" the "country of it."[54] Hodge at Princeton in the North had a similar outlook. The South, admitted Hodge, wanted to preserve a slave system "fraught with evil." This conduct provoked "the Divine pleasure." The end result was the "universal overthrow of slavery within the limits of the United States." "This," he asserted, "is one of the most momentous events in the history of the world." What lay behind all that had happened? Hodge concluded, "That it was the design of God to bring about this event cannot be doubted."[55]

Lincoln had told Joshua Speed "what he desired to live for." He desired "to link his name with something that would redound to the interest of his fellow man."[56] This indeed is what he did. Since Lincoln freed the slaves, one could well argue that the Civil War fulfilled the original American vision of a society reflecting divine moral principles. There indeed were Union soldiers who volunteered with the intention of destroying the "slave power" and purifying the nation of a great evil.[57] It has been rightfully said that there were Christian soldiers in the North who liked to think that their "fiery trial" in war had brought cleansing so that the nation could now be the "city upon a hill," "a light and example to the world."[58]

Calvin on the Issue of Slavery

Hodge in his reflections showed continuity with the thought of Calvin who spoke about "the common and general law of all nations" in which "slaves with their children should continue bound forever, so that the father had no more right to his own children than had a horse (as you might say) or any other beast over their offspring."[59] Calvin repudiated the moral wrong of such a heartless system. "If we consider what the right of nature was," Calvin stated, "we shall always say it was a thing totally against nature. For we are all fashioned after the image of God."[60]

At the same time, we need to recognize that for Calvin slavery was not evil per se in all instances.[61] It was not in his judgment intrinsically wicked in every case. He drew this conclusion from the fact that Paul sent the runaway slave, Onesimus, back to his owner, Philemon. "We hence see," he said, "that the thing in itself is not unlawful."[62]

Calvin, nevertheless, would have dissented from the view of Benjamin Morgan Palmer that slavery was a positive good, a sacred trust, an institution that could rightfully be extended into the territories. He likewise would have disagreed with Northern Copperheads who believed that slavery was "consistent with natural justice."[63] Calvin wrote, "Slavery is contrary to that right government which is most desirable."[64] As he reflected on the Republic of Geneva and other European nations of his time, Calvin reminded his congregation, "We have great cause to praise God for taking away such bondage from among men."[65] "Our condition," he affirmed, "is better, that is, in having hired servants and not slaves."[66] Lincoln stood with Calvin at this point.[67] To use the language of the jurist David Davis, Lincoln "loved the struggling masses—all uprising towards a higher Civilization had his assent & his prayer."[68]

The Cornerstone of the Confederacy

Calvin would have rejected the thinking of Alexander Stephens, the vice president of the Confederate States of America, expressed on March 21, 1861, in Savannah, Georgia, almost six weeks after the new republic had been established.[69] In what has been called the "Cornerstone Speech," Stephens rejected the idea of "a principle founded in nature, the principle of the equality of men."[70] The "cornerstone" of the Confederacy, he said, rested upon "the great truth, that the negro is not equal to the white man; that slavery—subordination to the superior race—is his natural and normal condition."[71] The place of "subordination" is "in conformity with the ordinance of the Creator."[72] Stephens asserted that the slavery of the African was imbedded in the natural order.[73]

Lincoln set forth a strikingly different view than that of Stephens. In 1858, he spoke about the *imago Dei* and the men who signed the Declaration of Independence, "In their enlightened belief, nothing stamped with the divine image and likeness was sent into the world to be trodden on, and degraded, and imbruted by its fellows." He then reflected upon the future: "They grasped not only the whole race of men then living, but they reached forward and seized upon the farthest posterity. They erected a beacon to guide their children and their children's children, and the countless myriads who should inhabit the earth in other ages."[74]

The True Order of Nature

The contrast between Stephens and the teaching of Calvin and Augustine is likewise stark. Calvin wrote about the natural order and the fact that it entailed equality and liberty for every member of the human race. "The order of nature," Calvin insisted, was such that "men were created for the purpose of cultivating mutual society between each other." "Liberty," he said, "was common to all" at creation. It was "not long after the deluge," however, that "the wickedness of man caused liberty" to "perish with respect to a great part of mankind." "An equality, as among brethren," though, "ought to have been retained."[75]

Augustine also discussed relationships and the "order of nature" that God prescribed at creation before man fell into sin. Equality between human beings was the divine intention.[76] "God created man," he said, to "have lordship" over the animals. "He did not wish the rational being, made in his own image, to have dominion over any but irrational creatures, not man over man."[77] "By nature, in the condition in which God made man, no man is the slave either of man or of sin."[78]

The thinking of Augustine would have resonated with Lincoln. The church father had asked, "Who would be capable of listing the number and gravity of the ills which abound in human society amid the distresses of our mortal condition?"[79] He would, as a seasoned lawyer, have well related to Augustine's description of cities as places "filled with civil lawsuits and criminal trials" and courtrooms as the arena of false witnesses.[80] He would have concurred with the thought that injustice was the reason that the world was the scene of "social and civil wars."[81] He would have identified with the perspective that the wise man "will rather lament the fact that he is faced with the necessity of just wars." As he explained, "For it is the injustice of the opposing side that lays on the wise man the duty of waging wars."[82]

Lincoln longed for a better day when the cause of God would be realized in the United States. He prayed for victory when Union forces met Lee and the Army of Northern Virginia in Pennsylvania on July 1–3, 1863. The president identified the cause of the North with the will of God. Said Lincoln, "I went into my room one day and locked the door and got down on my knees before Almighty God and prayed to him mightily for victory at Gettysburg. I told him this was his war and our cause, his cause, but that we couldn't stand another Fredericksburg or Chancellorsville." He likewise made a vow to God: "I then and there made a solemn vow to Almighty God that if he would stand by our boys at Gettysburg, I would stand by him. And he did, and I will."[83]

Several months later, on November 19, 1863, in his Gettysburg Address, he spoke about the better day for which he yearned. He called the nation to be fully "dedicated to the proposition that all men are created equal." He expressed his desire that the nation "under God" would have "a new birth of freedom."[84] In his Second Inaugural, he expressed his vision in one concluding sentence of a nation reflecting love, justice, and peace: "With malice toward none; with charity for all; with firmness in the right, as God gives us to see the right, let us strive on to finish the work we are in; to bind up the nation's wounds; for him who shall have borne the battle, and for his widow, and his orphan—to do all which may achieve and cherish a just and lasting peace among ourselves, and with all nations."[85]

The President's Desire to See Jerusalem

Lincoln, though, understood that ultimate happiness is not to be found in this world. He would not have disputed the statement that "human life is compelled to be wretched by all the grievous evils of this world."[86] "In this sad world," said Lincoln, "sorrow comes to all."[87] He stood with those who "desire a better, that is, a heavenly country."[88] He had spoken of heaven as the place in which there would be "a joyous meeting with the many loved ones gone before."

"Through the help of God" he expressed his desire to join them before long.[89] On that fateful Good Friday, Lincoln displayed a cheerfulness that amazed his wife Mary. On that afternoon, he told her, "We must both, be more cheerful in the future."[90] That evening the president accompanied his wife and two guests to Ford's Theatre where Lincoln referred to, as Augustine put it, "the name of the City" which "has a mystic significance."[91] The president told Mary in a suggestive and loaded statement that he would like to "visit the Holy Land and see those places hallowed by the footsteps of the Savior" and that "there was no city on earth he so much desired to see as Jerusalem."[92]

Augustine articulated similar sentiments of a better world that is to come. He attempted to give assurance to the slaves of his time and succeeding generations of a better day in the future. Slavery and injustice will give place to love and peace in the Eternal Kingdom. He said concerning slaves in the present fallen world, "If they cannot be set free by their masters, they themselves may thus make their slavery, in a sense, free, by serving not with the slyness of fear, but with the fidelity of affection, until all injustice disappears and all human lordship and power is annihilated, and God is all in all."[93] God will be "the source" of our "satisfaction." He "shall be everything that men can honourably desire: life, health, food, wealth, glory, honour, peace, and every blessing." We may live with joy in the present knowing that "there will be true peace, where none will suffer attack from within himself nor from any foe outside."[94]

Conclusion

Few lives have been so utterly remarkable. The boy who spent his early years living in the backwoods of Kentucky and Indiana in small cabins with dirt floors was elevated as a man to the heights of political power. He became, as William Herndon put it, the "Chief Magistrate of the greatest nation of modern times."[1] The United States at the time was the largest slaveholding nation in the world, and he was the central figure in a chain of events that resulted in the Thirteenth Amendment which put an end to the institution of slavery in America.

The nation underwent a revolution, and Lincoln himself experienced inward transformation. His friends and neighbors in New Salem and Springfield had been shocked by his attacks upon Scripture arising out of a heart of bold infidelity. But tragedy and suffering came and chiseled away the hardness and arrogance. Lincoln came to love the gospel and humbled himself to receive the ministry of the Reverend Phineas Gurley at New York Avenue Presbyterian Church in Washington. When the Union forces met the Confederates at Gettysburg, Lincoln got down on his knees and prayed. He vowed to stand by God, if God would stand by the boys at Gettysburg. He later acknowledged that God did stand by the Union boys and that he, Lincoln, was determined to stand by God.[2]

Many historians contend that Lincoln was the preeminent president of the United States.[3] In what did his greatness consist? His integrity may well be his fundamental quality. This was the thing that Reverend Gurley singled out in his funeral sermon declaring of the fallen president, "His integrity was thorough, all pervading, all controlling, and incorruptible."[4] His uprightness had many facets. There was in him, as Herndon affirmed, an "exalted sense of right and equity."[5] This was the reason for his opposition to slavery, what he regarded as a merciless system of labor founded in the selfishness of man's nature. There was his commitment to honesty. His advice to those considering law as a profession was this: "Resolve to be honest at all events; and if in your judgment you cannot be an honest lawyer, resolve to be honest without being a lawyer."[6]

There was also his deep humility. Joshua Speed had maintained of him and his rise to the presidency, "None but a genius could have accomplished so much."[7] Lincoln, on the other hand, directed attention away from himself: "It has pleased Almighty God to place me in my present position."[8] There was his legendary kindness and mercy not only for the slaves, but even for the defeated Confederates. "I want no one punished."[9] This was his desire, and it was carried out in the actions of General Grant at Appomattox Court House.

What can we learn from Lincoln for our time?

He would turn us away from an approach of unquestioning deference to a majority decision of the Supreme Court. Lincoln knew that justices are not by nature any more honest than other men. He would therefore warn us against equating morality with decisions rendered by the Supreme Court. He would present the hope that erroneous and even immoral decisions of the High Court might well be reversed upon further reflection.

Lincoln would call upon us to reject the view that moral legitimacy is based upon a majority vote in the body politic, the result of whatever side is stronger at any given moment on a specific issue. Rather, moral legitimacy in legislation depends on whether or not it conforms to natural law, the law above the law. We must look, he said, to the Declaration of Independence to find core transcendent moral principles. It provides "the moral lights" of self-evident truth to guide our way.[10] The fundamental perspectives are these: "All men are created equal." And secondly, "they are endowed by their Creator with certain unalienable Rights." Three paramount human rights are then listed: "Among these are Life, Liberty, and the pursuit of Happiness." Legislation that tramples upon such rights is tyrannical.[11] To use the language of Calvin, laws that are "abhorrent not only to all justice, but also to all humanity and gentleness" are not really to be regarded as laws. Law "must be in conformity to" the "perpetual rule of love."[12]

Lincoln would insist upon the reality and compulsory force of natural law. As Luther noted in his commentary on Romans 2:15, natural law "is inscribed in the hearts of all men, Jews as well as Gentiles, and it obligates every person."[13] Its content, he explained, is the Golden Rule as articulated by Jesus in the Sermon on the Mount. Indeed, Lincoln as president made every effort to follow the fundamental principle of ethical behavior: "Do unto others as ye would they should do unto you."[14] He believed that a society that remembered the Golden Rule in its law would necessarily have to oppose every threat to the life of every human being, as well as every encroachment upon their liberty and their right to pursue happiness.

Appendix A

Second Inaugural Address

Washington, D.C.
March 4, 1865

Fellow-countrymen: At this second appearing to take the oath of the presidential office, there is less occasion for an extended address than there was at the first. Then a statement, somewhat in detail, of a course to be pursued, seemed fitting and proper. Now, at the expiration of four years, during which public declarations have been constantly called forth on every point and phase of the great contest which still absorbs the attention and engrosses the energies of the nation, little that is new could be presented. The progress of our arms, upon which all else chiefly depends, is as well known to the public as to myself; and it is, I trust, reasonably satisfactory and encouraging to all. With high hope for the future, no prediction in regard to it is ventured.

On the occasion corresponding to this four years ago, all thoughts were anxiously directed to an impending civil war. All dreaded it—all sought to avert it. While the inaugural address was being delivered from this place, devoted all together to saving the Union without war, insurgent agents were in the city seeking to destroy it without war—seeking to dissolve the Union, and divide effects, by negotiation. Both parties deprecated war; but one of them would make war rather than let the nation survive; and the other would accept war rather than let it perish. And the war came.

One-eighth of the whole population were colored slaves, not distributed generally over the Union, but localized in the Southern part of it. These slaves constituted a peculiar and powerful interest. All knew that this interest was, somehow, the cause of the war. To strengthen, perpetuate, and extend this interest was the object for which the insurgents would rend the Union, even by war; while the government claimed no right to do more than to restrict the territorial enlargement of it.

Neither party expected for the war the magnitude or the duration which it has already attained. Neither anticipated that the cause of the conflict might cease with, or even before, the conflict itself should cease. Each looked for an easier triumph, and a result less fundamental and astounding. Both read the same Bible, and pray to the same God; and each invokes his aid against the other. It may seem strange that any men should dare to ask a just God's assistance in wringing their bread from the sweat of other men's faces; but let us judge not, that we be not judged. The prayers of both could not be answered—that of neither has been answered fully.

The Almighty has his own purposes. "Woe unto the world because of offenses! for it must needs be that offenses come; but woe to that man by whom the offense cometh." If we shall suppose that American slavery is one of those offenses which, in the providence of God, must needs come, but which, having continued through his appointed time, he now wills to remove, and that he gives to both North and South this terrible war, as the woe due to those by whom the offense came, shall we discern therein any departure from those divine attributes which the believers in a living God always ascribe to him? Fondly do we hope—fervently do we pray—that this mighty scourge of war may speedily pass away. Yet, if God wills that it continue until all the wealth piled by the bondman's two hundred and fifty years of unrequited toil shall be sunk, and every drop of blood drawn with the lash shall be paid by another drawn with sword, as was said three thousand years ago, so still it must be said, "The judgments of the Lord are true and righteous altogether."

With malice toward none; with charity for all; with firmness in the right, as God gives us to see the right, let us strive on to finish the work we are in; to bind up the nation's wounds; to care for him who shall have borne the battle, and for his widow, and his orphan—to do all which may achieve and cherish a just and lasting peace among ourselves, and with all nations.

Appendix B

Phineas Gurley's White House Funeral Sermon

Washington, D.C.
April 19, 1865

AS WE STAND HERE TODAY, MOURNERS AROUND THIS COFFIN AND AROUND THE LIFELESS REMAINS OF OUR BELOVED CHIEF MAGISTRATE, WE RECOGNIZE AND WE ADORE THE SOVEREIGNTY OF GOD. His throne is in the heavens, and His kingdom ruleth over all. He hath done, and He hath permitted to be done, whatsoever He pleased. "Clouds and darkness are round about Him; righteousness and judgment are the habitation of His throne." His way is in the sea, and His path in the great waters, and His footsteps are not known. "Canst thou by searching find out God? Canst thou find out the Almighty unto perfection? It is as high as heaven; what canst thou do? Deeper than hell; what canst thou know? The measure thereof is longer than the earth, and broader than the sea. If He cut off, and shut up, or gather together, then who can hinder Him? For He knoweth vain men; he seeth wickedness also; will He not then consider it?"—We bow before His infinite majesty. We bow, we weep, we worship.

> "Where reason fails, with all her powers,
> There faith prevails, and love adores."

It was a cruel, cruel hand, that dark hand of the assassin, which smote our honored, wise, and noble President, and filled the land with sorrow. But above and beyond that hand is another which we must see and acknowledge. It is the chastening hand of a wise and a faithful Father. He gives us this bitter cup. And the cup that our Father hath given us, shall we not drink it?

> "God of the just, Thou gavest us the cup
> We yield to thy behest, and drink it up."

"Whom the Lord loveth He chasteneth." O how these blessed words have cheered and strengthened and sustained us through all these long and weary years of civil strife, while our friends and brothers on so many ensanguined fields, were falling and dying for the cause of Liberty and Union! Let them cheer, and strengthen, and sustain us to-day. True, this new sorrow and chastening has come in such an hour and in such a way as we thought not, and it bears the impress of a rod that is very heavy, and of a mystery that is very deep. That such a life should be sacrificed, at such a time, by such a foul and diabolical agency; that the man at the head of the nation, whom the people had learned to trust with a confiding and a loving confidence, and upon whom more than upon any other were centered, under God, our best hopes for the true and speedy pacification of the country, the restoration of the Union, and the return of harmony and love; that he should be taken from us, and taken just as the prospect of peace was brightly opening upon our torn and bleeding country, and just as he was beginning to be animated and gladdened with the hope of ere long enjoying with the people the blessed fruit and reward of his and their toil, and care, and patience, and self-sacrificing devotion to the interests of Liberty and the Union—O it is a mysterious and a most afflicting visitation! But it is our Father in heaven, the God of our fathers, and our God, who permits us to be so suddenly and sorely smitten; and we know that His judgments are right, and that in faithfulness He has afflicted us. In the midst of our rejoicings we needed this stroke, this dealing, this discipline; and therefore He has sent it. Let us remember, our affliction has not come forth out of the dust, and our trouble has not sprung out of the ground. Through and beyond all second causes let us look, and see the sovereign permissive agency of the great First Cause. It is His prerogative to bring light out of darkness and good out of evil. Surely the wrath of man shall praise Him, and the remainder of wrath He will restrain. In the light of a clearer day we may yet see that the wrath which planned and perpetuated the death of the President, was overruled by Him whose judgements are unsearchable, and His ways are past finding out, for the highest welfare of all those interests which are so dear to the Christian patriot and philanthropist, and for which a loyal people have made such an unexampled sacrifice of treasure and of blood. Let us not be faithless, but believing.

"Blind unbelief is prone to err,
And scan His work in vain;
God is his own interpreter
And He will make it plain."

We will wait for his interpretation, and we will wait in faith, nothing doubting. He who has led so well, and defended and prospered us so wonderfully during the last four years of toil, and struggle, and sorrow, will not forsake us now. He may chasten, but He will not destroy. He may purify us more and more in the furnace of trial, but He will not consume us. No, no! He has chosen us as He did his people of old in the furnace of affliction, and He has said of us as He said of them, "This people have I formed for myself; they shall show forth My praise." Let our principal anxiety now be that this new sorrow may be a sanctified sorrow; that it may lead us to deeper repentance, to a more humbling sense of our dependence upon God, and to the more unreserved consecration of ourselves and all that we have to the cause of truth and justice, of law and order, of liberty and good government, of pure and undefiled religion. Then, though weeping may endure for a night, joy will come in the morning. Blessed be God! despite of this great and sudden and temporary darkness, the morning has begun to dawn—the morning of a bright and glorious day, such as our country has never seen. That day will come and not tarry, and the death of a hundred Presidents and their Cabinets can never, never prevent it. While we are thus hopeful, however, let us also be humble. The occasion calls us to prayerful and tearful humiliation. It demands us that we lie low, very low, before Him who has smitten us for our sins. O that all our rulers and all our people may bow in the dust to-day beneath the chastening hand of God! and may their voices go up to Him as one voice, and their hearts go up to Him as one heart, pleading with Him for mercy, for grace to sanctify our great and sore bereavement, and for wisdom to guide us in this our time of need. Such a united cry and pleading will not be in vain. It will enter into the ear and heart of Him who sits upon the throne, and He will say to us, as to His ancient Israel, "In a little wrath I hid my face from thee for a moment: but with everlasting kindness will I have mercy upon thee, said the Lord, thy Redeemer."

I have said that the people confided in the late lamented President with a full and a loving confidence. Probably no man since the days of Washington was ever so deeply and firmly embedded and enshrined in the very hearts of the people as Abraham Lincoln. Nor was it a mistaken confidence and love. He deserved it well—deserved it all. He merited it by his character, by his acts, and by the whole tenor, and tone, and spirit of his life. He was simple and sincere, plain and honest, truthful and just, benevolent and kind. His perceptions were quick and clear, his judgments were calm and accurate, and his purposes were good and pure beyond a question. Always and everywhere he aimed and endeavored to be right and to do right. His integrity was thorough, all-pervading, all-controlling, and incorruptible. It was the same in every place and every relation, in the consideration and the control of matters great or small, the same firm and steady principle of power and beauty that shed a clear and crowning lustre upon all his other excellencies of mind and heart, and recommended him to his fellow citizens as *the* man, who, in a time of unexampled peril, when the very life of the nation was at stake, should be chosen to occupy, in the country and for the country, its highest post of power and responsibility. How wisely and well, how purely and faithfully, how firmly and steadily, how justly and successfully he did occupy that post and meet its grave demands in circumstances of surpassing trial and difficulty, is known to you all, known to the country and the world. He comprehended from the first the perils to which treason has exposed the freest and best Government on the earth, the vast interests of Liberty and humanity that were to be saved or lost forever in the urgent impending conflict; he rose to the dignity and momentousness of the occasion, saw his duty as the Chief Magistrate of a great and imperilled people, and he determined to do his duty, and his whole duty, seeking the guidance and leaning upon the arm of Him of whom it is written, "He giveth power to the faint, and to them that have no might He increaseth strength." Yes, he leaned upon His arm. He recognized and received the truth that the "kingdom is the Lord's, and He is the governor among the nations." He remembered that "God is in history," and he felt that nowhere had His hand and His mercy been so marvelously conspicuous as in the history of this nation. He hoped and he prayed that that same hand would continue to guide us, and that same mercy continue to abound to us in the time of our greatest need. I speak what I know, and testify what I have often heard him say, when I affirm that that guidance and mercy were the props on which he humbly and habitually leaned; they were the best hope he had for himself and for his country. Hence, when he was leaving his home in Illinois, and coming to this city to take his seat in the executive chair of a disturbed and troubled nation, he said to the old and tried friends who gathered tearfully around him and bade him farewell, "I leave you with this request: *pray for me*." They did pray for him; and millions of other people prayed for him; nor did they pray in vain. Their prayer was heard, and the answer appears in all his subsequent history; it shines forth with a heavenly radiance in the whole course and tenor of his administration, from its commencement to its close. God raised him up for a great and glorious mission, furnished him for his work, and aided him in its accomplishment. Nor was it merely by strength of mind, and honesty of heart, and purity and pertinacity of purpose, that He furnished him; in addition to these things, He gave him a calm and abiding confidence in the overruling providence of God and in the ultimate triumph of truth and righteousness through the power and the blessing of God. This confidence strengthened him in all his hours of anxiety and toil, and inspired him with calm and cheering hope when others were inclining to despondency and gloom. Never shall I forget the emphasis and the deep emotion with which he said in this very room, to a company of clergymen and others, who called to pay him their respects in the darkest days of our civil conflict: "Gentlemen, my hope of success in this great and terrible struggle rests on that immutable foundation, the justice and goodness of God. And when events are very threatening and prospects very dark, I still hope that in some way which man can not see all will be well in the end, because our cause is just, and God is on our side." Such was his sublime and holy faith, and it was an anchor to his soul, both sure and steadfast. It made him firm and strong. It emboldened him in the pathway of duty, however rugged and perilous it might be. It made him valiant for the right; for the cause of God and humanity, and it held him in a steady, patient, and unswerving adherence to a policy of administration which he thought, and which we all now think, both God and humanity required him to adopt. We admired him and loved him on many accounts—for strong and various reasons: we admired his childlike simplicity, his freedom from guile and deceit, his staunch and sterling integrity, his kind and forgiving temper, his industry and patience, his persistent, self-sacrificing devotion to all the duties of his eminent position, from the least to the greatest; his readiness to hear and consider the cause of the poor and the humble, the suffering and the oppressed; his charity toward those who questioned the correctness of his opinions and the wisdom of his policy; his wonderful skill in reconciling differences among the friends of the Union, leading them away from abstractions, and inducing them to work together and harmoniously for the common weal; his true and enlarged philanthropy, that knew no distinction of color or race, but regarded all men as brethren, and endowed alike by their Creator "with certain inalienable rights, among which are life, Liberty, and the pursuit of happiness"; his inflexible purpose that what freedom had gained in our terrible civil strife should never be lost, and that the end of the war should be the end of slavery, and, as a consequence, of rebellion; his readiness to spend and be spent for the attainment of such a triumph—a triumph, the blessed fruits of which shall be as widespreading as the earth and as enduring as the sun:—all these things commanded and fixed our admiration and the admiration of the world, and stamped upon his character and life the unmistakable impress of *greatness.* But more sublime than any or all of these, more holy and influential, more beautiful, and strong, and sustaining, was *his abiding confidence in God and in the final triumph of truth and righteousness through Him and for His sake.* This was his noblest virtue, his grandest principle, the secret alike of his strength, his patience, and his success. And this, it seems to me, after being near him steadily, and with him often, for more than four years, is the principle by which, more than by any other, "he, being dead, yet speaketh." Yes; by his steady enduring confidence in God, and in the complete ultimate success of the cause of God, which is the cause of humanity, more than by any other way, does he now speak to us and to the nation he loved and served so well. By this he speaks to his successor in office, and charges him to "have faith in God." By this he speaks to the members of his cabinet, the men with whom he counselled so often and was associated so long, and he charges them to "have faith in God." By this he speaks to the officers and men of our noble army and navy, and, as they stand at their posts of duty and peril, he charges them to "have faith in God." By this he speaks to all who occupy positions of influence and authority in these sad and troublous times, and he charges them all to "have faith in God." By this he speaks to this great people as they sit in sackcloth to-day, and weep for him with a bitter wailing, and refuse to be comforted, and he charges them to "have faith in

God." And by this he *will* speak through the ages and to all rulers and peoples in every land, and his message to them will be, "Cling to Liberty and right; battle for them; bleed for them; die for them, if need be; and have confidence in God." O that the voice of this testimony may sink down into our hearts to-day and every day, and into the heart of the nation, and exert its appropriate influence upon our feelings, our faith, our patience, and our devotion to the cause of freedom and humanity—a cause dearer to us than before, because consecrated by the blood of its most conspicuous defender, its wisest and most fondly-trusted friend.

He is dead; but the God in whom he trusted lives, and He can guide and strengthen his successor, as He guided and strengthened him. He is dead; but the memory of his virtues, of his wise and patriotic counsels and labors, of his calm and steady faith in God lives, is precious, and will be a power for good in the country quite down to the end of time. He is dead; but the cause he so ardently loved, so ably, patiently, faithfully represented and defended—not for himself only, not for us only, but for all people in all their coming generations, till time shall be no more—that cause survives his fall, and will survive it. The light of its brightening prospects flashes cheeringly to-day athwart the gloom occasioned by his death, and the language of God's united providences is telling us that, though the friends of Liberty die, Liberty itself is immortal. There is no assassin strong enough and no weapon deadly enough to quench its inextinguishable life, or arrest its onward march to the conquest and empire of the world. This is our confidence, and this is our consolation, as we weep and mourn to-day. Though our beloved President is slain, our beloved country is saved. And so we sing of mercy as well as of judgment. Tears of gratitude mingle with those of sorrow. While there is darkness, there is also the dawning of a brighter, happier day upon our stricken and weary land. God be praised that our fallen Chief lived long enough to see the day dawn and the daystar of joy and peace arise upon the nation. He saw it, and he was glad. Alas! alas! He only saw the *dawn*. When the *sun* has risen, full-orbed and glorious, and a happy reunited people are rejoicing in its light—alas! alas! it will shine upon his grave. But that grave will be a precious and a consecrated spot. The friends of Liberty and of the Union will repair to it in years and ages to come, to pronounce the memory of its occupant blessed, and, gathering from his very ashes, and the rehearsal of his deeds and virtues, fresh incentives to patriotism, they will there renew their vows of fidelity to their country and their God.

And now I know not that I can more appropriately conclude this discourse, which is but a sincere and simple utterance of the heart, than by addressing to our departed President, with some slight modification, the language which Tacitus, in his life of Agricola, addresses to his venerable and departed father-in-law: "With you we may now congratulate; you are blessed, not only because your life was a career of glory, but because you were released, when, your country safe, it was happiness to die. We have lost a parent, and, in our distress, it is now an addition to our heartfelt sorrow that we had it not in our power to commune with you on the bed of languishing, and receive your last embrace. Your dying words would have been ever dear to us; your commands we should have treasured up, and graved them on our hearts. This sad comfort we have lost, and the wound for that reason, pierces deeper. From the world of spirits behold your desolate family and people; exalt our minds from fond regret and unavailing grief to contemplation of your virtues. Those we must not lament; it were impiety to sully them with a tear. To cherish their memory, to embalm them with our praises, and, so far as we can, to emulate your bright example, will be the truest mark of our respect, the best tribute we can offer. Your wife will thus preserve the memory of the best of husbands, and thus your children will prove their filial piety.

By dwelling constantly on your words and actions, they will have an illustrious character before their eyes, and, not content with the bare image of your mortal frame, they will have what is more valuable—the form and features of your mind. Busts and statues, like their originals, are frail and perishable. The soul is formed of finer elements, and its inward from is not to be expressed by the hand of an artist with unconscious matter—our manners and our morals may in some degree trace the resemblance. All of you that gained our love and raised our admiration still subsists, and will ever subsist, preserved in the minds of men, the register of ages, and records of fame. Others, who had figured on the stage of life and were worthies of a former day, will sink, for want of a faithful historian, into the common lot of oblivion, inglorious and unremembered; but you, our lamented friend and head, delineated with truth, and fairly consigned to posterity, will survive yourself, and triumph over the injuries of time."

Endnotes

Introduction

1 Allen C. Guelzo, *Abraham Lincoln as a Man of Ideas* (Carbondale: Southern Illinois University Press, 2009), 80.

2 Abraham Lincoln, "Protest Entered in the Illinois Legislature," in *Lincoln Speeches*, ed. Allen C. Guelzo (New York: Penguin Books, 2012), 4–5.

3 Willmore Kendall and George W. Carey, *The Basic Symbols of the American Political Tradition* (Washington, D.C.: Catholic University Press, 1995), ix.

4 Robert R. Reilly, *America on Trial: A Defense of the Founding* (San Francisco: Ignatius Press, 2020), 15, 66–107.

Chapter 1

1 *Recollected Words of Abraham Lincoln*, ed. Don E. Fehrenbacher and Virginia Fehrenbacher (Stanford, CA: Stanford University Press, 1996), 510.

2 Richard Carwardine, *Lincoln: A Life of Purpose and Power* (New York: Alfred A. Knopf, 2006), 49. Cf., *Recollected Words of Abraham Lincoln*, 507; William Lee Miller, *Lincoln's Virtues: An Ethical Biography* (New York: Alfred A. Knopf, 2003), 4.

3 Stephen B. Oates, *Abraham Lincoln: The Man behind the Myths* (New York: Harper & Row, 1984), 34, 39–40.

4 Garry Wills, *Lincoln at Gettysburg: The Words That Remade America* (New York: Simon & Schuster, 1992), 36; Richard Carwardine, *Lincoln's Sense of Humor* (Carbondale, IL: Southern Illinois University Press, 2017), 8; John Dos Passos, "Lincoln and His Almost Chosen People," in *Lincoln and the Gettysburg Address*, ed. Allan Nevins (Urbana, IL: University of Illinois Press, 1964), 19.

5 William H. Herndon and Jesse W. Weik, *Herndon's Lincoln*, ed. Douglas L. Wilson and Rodney O. Davis (Urbana and Chicago: University of Illinois Press, 2006), 408.

6 Miller comments, "The Whig Party was born in opposition to Andrew Jackson and the Jacksonian Democrats." *Lincoln's Virtues*, 100.

7 In his first political statement in March 1832, Lincoln announced his commitment to "the public utility of internal improvements." The Sangamon River, he said, needed to be "greatly improved by art." He then promised, "If elected, any measure in the legislature having this for its object, which may appear judicious, will meet my approbation, and shall receive my support." "To the People of Sangamo County," in *Lincoln Speeches*, ed. Allen C. Guelzo (New York: Penguin Books, 2012), 1–2.

8 Allen C. Guelzo, *Abraham Lincoln: Redeemer President* (Grand Rapids and Cambridge, UK: William B. Eerdmans, 1999), 57, specifies that Lincoln wanted a national bank "to create a dependable and uniform system of national investment, currency, and finance."

9 Lincoln first ran for the Illinois House of Representatives in 1832 when he was twenty-three years old. He did not win, but he did win in 1834, 1836, 1838, and 1840. He also won in 1854, but then resigned.

10 Abraham Lincoln, *The Lincoln-Douglas Debates*, ed. Rodney O. Davis and Douglas L. Wilson (Urbana and Chicago: University of Illinois Press, 2008), 193. Cf., Carwardine, *Lincoln: A Life of Purpose and Power*, 21–22.

11 Herndon and Weik, *Herndon's Lincoln*, 357.

12 Lincoln, *The Lincoln-Douglas Debates*, 222.

13 Lincoln, *The Lincoln-Douglas Debates*, 223.

14 Mark A. Noll, *The Civil War as a Theological Crisis* (Chapel Hill: University of North Carolina Press, 2006), 1.

15 John R. McKivigan, *The War against Proslavery Religion: Abolitionism and the Northern Churches, 1830–1865* (Ithaca and London: Cornell University Press, 1984), 49. Cf., Irving Stoddard Kull, "Presbyterian Attitudes toward Slavery," *Church History* 7, no. 2 (June 1938): 106.

16 Joseph A. Conforti, *Samuel Hopkins and the New Divinity Movement: Calvinism, the Congregational Ministry, and Reform in New England Between the Great Awakenings* (Eugene, OR: Wipf & Stock, 1981), 125–141.

17 Samuel Hopkins, "A Dialogue Concerning the Slavery of the Africans, Showing It to Be the Duty and Interest of the American Colonies to Emancipate All

Their African Slaves," in *The New England Theology*, ed. Douglas A. Sweeney and Allen C. Guelzo (Eugene, OR: Wipf & Stock, 2015), 152.

18 Samuel Hopkins, *A Discourse upon the Slave-Trade, and the Slavery of the Africans* (Providence, 1793), 18. Mark A. Noll, *America's God: From Jonathan Edwards to Abraham Lincoln* (Oxford: Oxford University Press, 2002), 271.

19 James H. Thornwell, "The Christian Doctrine of Slavery," in *The Collected Writings of James Henley Thornwell*, vol. 4 (Edinburgh: Banner of Truth, 1974), 430. Cf., Ronald C. White, *Lincoln in Private: What His Most Personal Reflections Tell Us About Our Greatest President* (New York: Random House, 2021), 106.

20 Harry S. Stout, *Upon the Altar of the Nation: A Moral History of the Civil War* (New York: Viking, 2006), 43. Lincoln reflected upon the view that slavery was a good thing saying. "As a *good* thing," he remarked, "slavery is strikingly peculiar, in this, that it is the only good thing which no man ever seeks the good of, *for himself*." Miller, *Lincoln's Virtues*, 280.

21 James P. Byrd, *A Holy Baptism of Fire and Blood: The Bible and the American Civil War* (New York: Oxford University Press, 2021), 100.

22 The Methodists and Baptists likewise divided over the issue of slavery. Cf., Byrd, *A Holy Baptism of Fire and Blood*, 27; Mark A. Noll, *A History of Christianity in the United States and Canada* (Grand Rapids: William B. Eerdmans, 1992), 316–317; James W. Silver, *Confederate Morale and Church Propaganda* (Tuscaloosa, AL: Confederate Publishing Company, 1957), 16; John Halsey Wood, "The 1861 Spring Resolutions: Charles Hodge, the American Union, and the Dissolution of the Old School Church," *Journal of Church and State* 47, no. 2 (Spring 2005): 372; Paul K. Conkin, *The Uneasy Center: Reformed Christianity in Antebellum America* (Chapel Hill and London: University of North Carolina Press, 1995), 250.

23 William Sweet states, "The split in the churches was not only the first break between the sections, but the chief cause of the final break." William W. Sweet, *The Story of Religion in America* (New York: Harper & Brothers, 1950), 312.

24 Noll, *The Civil War as a Theological Crisis*, 75, focuses upon "the conflict in understanding providence" when it came to specific events during the course of the war. We are seeking to underscore the unity that existed among the Reformed in the eighteenth and nineteenth centuries with respect to the biblical doctrine of providence.

25 All citations from the "The Westminster Confession of Faith" are from *The Creeds of Christendom*, vol. 3, ed. Philip Schaff (Grand Rapids: Baker Book House, 1990), 600–73.

26 American Presbyterianism divided in 1837 between the New School and the Old School. While New School Presbyterianism embraced a modified Calvinist theology, the Old School insisted upon close adherence to the theology of the Westminster Standards. The Old School and the New School of the PCUSA reunited in 1869.

27 Kendall and Carey, *The Basic Symbols of the American Political Tradition*, ix.

28 "Mayflower Compact," in *The American Republic: Primary Sources*, ed. Bruce Frohnen (Indianapolis: Liberty Fund, 2002), 11. The Mayflower Compact was signed by the Pilgrims on board the *Mayflower*.

29 "Fundamental Orders of Connecticut," in *The American Republic: Primary Sources*, ed. Bruce Frohnen (Indianapolis: Liberty Fund, 2002), 12.

30 "The Declaration of Independence," in *The American Republic: Primary Sources*, ed. Bruce Frohnen (Indianapolis: Liberty Fund, 2002), 191.

31 "The Constitution of the United States of America," in *The American Republic: Primary Sources*, ed. Bruce Frohnen (Indianapolis: Liberty Fund, 2002), 239.

32 George Washington, "First Inaugural Address," in *An American Primer*, ed. Daniel J. Boorstin (New York: Mentor, 1966), 192.

33 John Calvin, *Commentary on the Gospel according to John*, vol. 18 (Grand Rapids: Baker Book House, 1979), 93.

34 John Calvin, *Institutes of the Christian Religion*, vol. 1, trans. Ford Lewis Battles (Philadelphia: Westminster Press, 1960), 278.

35 John Calvin, *Commentaries on the Epistle of Paul to the Ephesians*, vol. 21 (Grand Rapids: Baker Book House, 1979), 212.

36 William Ames, *The Marrow of Theology* (Grand Rapids: Baker Books, 1968), 78.

37 John Calvin, "Dedicatory Epistle to Simon Grynaeus," *Commentaries on the Epistle of Paul the Apostle to the Romans*, vol. 19 (Grand Rapids: Baker Book House, 1979), xxvii.

Chapter 2

1 Luke E. Harlow, "Slavery, Race, and Political Ideology in the White Christian South before and after the Civil War," in *Religion and American Politics: From the Colonial Period to the Present*, ed. Mark A. Noll and Luke E. Harlow, 2d ed. (Oxford and New York: Oxford University Press, 2007), 204.

2 James M. McPherson, *For Cause and Comrades: Why Men Fought in the Civil War* (New York and Oxford: Oxford University Press, 1997), 19–20, cites a number of documents from Confederate volunteers who fought for the purpose of defending the institution of slavery in the South.

3 Benjamin M. Palmer, *The Life and Letters of James Henley Thornwell* (Edinburgh: Banner of Truth, 1974), 342–43. It has been estimated that slightly more than fifty percent of the ministers in Beaufort, Columbia, and Spartanburg, South Carolina, owned slaves. Mitchell Snay, *Gospel of Disunion: Religion and Separation in the Antebellum South* (Cambridge: Cambridge University Press, 1993), 76.

4 James H. Thornwell, "Sermon on National Sins," in *The Collected Writings of James Henley Thornwell*, vol. 4 (Edinburgh: Banner of Truth, 1974), 539.

5 Reverend Thomas Smyth declared that the South had "an organized system of labor, for the benefit of the world, and a blessing to themselves while imparting civil, social, and religious blessings to their slaves." Silver, *Confederate Morale and Church Propaganda*, 30.

6 Douglas F. Kelly, "Robert Lewis Dabney," in *Southern Reformed Theology*, ed. David F. Wells (Grand Rapids: Baker Book House, 1989), 37.

7 Sean Michael Lucas, *Robert Lewis Dabney: A Southern Presbyterian Life* (Philipsburg, NJ: Presbyterian & Reformed), 31.

8 Robert L. Fern, *Jonathan Edwards the Younger, 1745–1801* (Grand Rapids: William B. Eerdmans, 1976), 95.

9 Steven E. Woodworth, *While God Is Marching On: The Religious World of Civil War Soldiers* (Lawrence, KS: University Press of Kansas, 2001), 18.

10 Bertram Wyatt-Brown, "Religion and the 'Civilizing Process' in the Early American South, 1600–1860," in *Religion and American Politics* (New York and Oxford: Oxford University Press, 1990), 177–78.

11 Kenneth P. Minkema and Harry S. Stout, "The Edwardsean Tradition and the Antislavery Debate, 1740–1865," *The Journal of American History* (June 2005): 53.

12 Jonathan Edwards Jr., "The Injustice and Impolicy of the Slave Trade and of Slavery," in *The New England Theology*, ed. Douglas A. Sweeney and Allen C. Guelzo (Eugene, OR: Wipf & Stock, 2015), 162.

13 Edwards Jr., "The Injustice and Impolicy of the Slave Trade and of Slavery," 161.

14 The New Divinity men were not the first intellectuals to speak against slavery. The Puritan Samuel Sewell in 1700 published *The Selling of* Joseph, the first publication against slavery that came out of New England.

15 Jonathan Edwards Jr., "The Necessity of the Belief of Christianity," in *Political Sermons of the Founding Era, 1730–1805*, ed. Ellis Sandoz (Indianapolis: Liberty Press, 1991), 1203.

16 Edwards Jr., "The Injustice and Impolicy of the Slave Trade and of Slavery," 163–64.

17 Heejoon Jeon, "Jonathan Edwards and the Anti-Slavery Movement," *Journal of the Evangelical Theological Society* 63, no. 4 (2020): 774, acknowledges that Samuel Hopkins is viewed by some historians as "the father of the antislavery movement in America."

18 Samuel Lincoln helped to build the Old Ship Church which is still being used today. See David S. Reynolds, *Abe: Abraham Lincoln in His Times* (New York: Penguin Books, 2020), 12–16.

19 Herndon and Weik, *Herndon's Lincoln*, 359.

20 James M. McPherson, *Abraham Lincoln* (Oxford: Oxford University Press, 2009), 64.

21 Allen C. Guelzo, *Fateful Lightning: A History of the Civil War & Reconstruction* (Oxford: Oxford University Press, 2012), 30.

22 Michael Burlingame, *The Inner World of Abraham Lincoln* (Urbana and Chicago: University of Illinois Press, 1994), 21.

23 Herndon and Weik, *Herndon's Lincoln*, 403–04. A journalist for the Chicago *Tribune* recorded these statements that Lincoln made at Edwardsville, Illinois, in the summer of 1858.

24 Abraham Lincoln, "Speech at Peoria," in *Lincoln Speeches*, ed. Allen C. Guelzo (New York: Penguin Books, 2012), 48.

25 Lincoln, "Speech at Peoria," 51. Lincoln rejected the view that "an action could be pure, disinterested, and wholly free from selfishness." Herndon and Weik, *Herndon's Lincoln*, 356.

26 Herndon and Weik, *Herndon's Lincoln*, 226.

27 Lincoln, *The Lincoln-Douglas Debates*, 19.

28 Carwardine, *Lincoln: A Life of Purpose and Power*, 75–76.

29 Herndon and Weik, *Herndon's Lincoln*, 388.

30 McPherson, *For Cause and Comrades*, 92, observes that the United States was "the world's most politicized and democratic country in the world in the mid-nineteenth century." The 1850s were a time when "highly charged partisan and ideological debates consumed the American polity."

31 Herndon and Weik, *Herndon's Lincoln*, 405.

32 Herndon and Weik, *Herndon's Lincoln*, 398.

33 Lincoln, "Speech at Peoria," 55.

34 Herndon and Weik, *Herndon's Lincoln*, 225.

35 Douglas made this statement at the First Debate in Ottawa with over ten thousand people in attendance. *The Lincoln-Douglas Debates*, 16.

36 Douglas used this expression in the Third Debate in Jonesboro, Illinois, on September 15, 1858, with only around fifteen hundred attendees. *The Lincoln-Douglas Debates*, 98.

37 Allen C. Guelzo, "Lincoln's Moral Constitution," *Word & World* 31, no. 2 (Spring 2011): 143–45, points out that Lincoln had no doubt about "a fundamental natural law that everyone could understand." Lincoln likewise believed that "mere majority rule cannot reverse natural law."

38 Harry V. Jaffa, *Crisis of the House Divided: An Interpretation of the Issues in the Lincoln-Douglas Debates* (Chicago and London: University of Chicago Press, 2009), xi.

39 Guelzo, *Abraham Lincoln as a Man of Ideas*, 83–84.

40 Abraham Lincoln, "House Divided" Speech, in *Lincoln Speeches*, ed. Allen C. Guelzo (New York: Penguin Books, 2012), 57.

41 Jaffa, *Crisis of the House Divided*, xi.

42 Abraham Lincoln, "Speech at Independence Hall," in *Lincoln Speeches*, ed. Allen C. Guelzo (New York: Penguin Books, 2012), 110–11.

43 Lincoln, *The Lincoln-Douglas Debates*, 270. Oates writes, "Lincoln idolized the Founding Fathers as apostles of liberty." *Abraham Lincoln: The Man behind the Myths*, 59.

44 Harold Holzer, *Lincoln and the Power of the Press* (New York: Simon & Schuster, 2014), 168, quotes from Lincoln's response to Dred Scott on June 26, 1857: "Our Declaration of Independence was held sacred by all, and thought to include all; but now, to aid in making the bondage of the negro universal and eternal, it is assailed."

45 Lincoln, *The Lincoln-Douglas Debates*, 271.

46 Lincoln, *The Lincoln-Douglas Debates*, 34.

47 Arthur Lehman Goodhart, "Lincoln and the Law," in *Lincoln and the Gettysburg Address*, ed. Allan Nevins (Urbana, IL: University of Illinois Press, 1964), 62. Lincoln in his one term in Congress from 1847 to 1849 voted several times for the Wilmot Proviso, which provided that slavery should be prohibited in any territory acquired from Mexico. McPherson, *Abraham Lincoln*, 13.

48 Lincoln, *The Lincoln-Douglas Debates*, 112. The Dred Scott decision provided the possibility that the northern states themselves might be open to slavery. Goodhart, "Lincoln and the Law," 62.

49 Lincoln, *The Lincoln-Douglas Debates*, 166.

50 Lincoln, *The Lincoln-Douglas Debates*, 32.

51 Lincoln, *The Lincoln-Douglas Debates*, 199.

52 Oates, *Abraham Lincoln: The Man behind the Myths*, 48.

53 Lincoln, *The Lincoln-Douglas Debates*, 32.

54 Lincoln, *The Lincoln-Douglas Debates*, 60.

55 Lincoln, *The Lincoln-Douglas Debates*, 200.

56 Lincoln, *The Lincoln-Douglas Debates*, 95.

57 Lincoln, *The Lincoln-Douglas Debates*, 210.

58 Robert P. George, "Lincoln on Judicial Despotism," *First Things* (February 2003): 38, recognizes that Lincoln believed in courts, but he did not venerate them. "Nor did he automatically identify what the courts did or said with 'the law.'"

59 Martin Bucer, *On the Kingdom of Christ*, ed. Wilhelm Pauck (Philadelphia: Westminster, 1969), 62.

60 John Calvin, *Commentary on the Book of Psalms*, vol. 5 (Grand Rapids: Baker Book House, 1979), 334.

61 Carwardine, *Lincoln's Sense of Humor*, 52–53.

62 Lincoln, in *The Lincoln-Douglas Debates*, 199.

63 Guelzo, *Abraham Lincoln as a Man of Ideas*, 82.

64 Abraham Kuyper, "Our Program," in *Political Order and Plural Structure of Society*, ed. James W. Skillen and Rockne M. McCarthy (Atlanta: Scholars, 1991), 255.

65 Kuyper, "Our Program," 247.

66 Lincoln, "Speech at Peoria," 52.

67 Miller, *Lincoln's Virtues*, 249.

68 Sidney Blumenthal, *A Self-Made Man: The Political Life of Abraham Lincoln, 1809-1849* (New York: Simon & Schuster, 2016), 189.

69 Herndon and Weik, *Herndon's Lincoln*, 395. T. Harry Williams, *Lincoln and His Generals* (New York: Random House, 1952), 25, states that George B. McClellan "always saw Lincoln as a person of inferior antecedents and abilities." McClellan actually voted for Douglas in the 1858 Senate race.

70 Blumenthal states concerning Douglas, "He relied on ranting, illogic, and invective, peppered with frequent use of the word 'nigger,' regularly accusing opponents of being their lovers." *A Self-Made Man*, 189.

71 Lincoln, *The Lincoln-Douglas Debates*, 210.

72 Goodhart, "Lincoln and the Law," 63.

73 Abraham Lincoln, "Address before the Young Men's Lyceum of Springfield, Illinois," in *Classics of American Political and Constitutional Thought*, vol. 1, ed. Scott J. Hammond, Kevin R. Hardwick, and Howard L. Lubert (Indianapolis and Cambridge: Hackett Publishing Company, 2007), 971.

74 Lincoln, "Address before the Young Men's Lyceum," 969.

75 Goodhart contends that the fundamental point for Lincoln was "the idea of law, on which all stable government must be based." Apart from "respect and obedience to the law" there must follow "either anarchy or tyranny." "Lincoln and the Law," 44.

76 Lincoln, "Address before the Young Men's Lyceum," 971.

77 Lincoln, "Address before the Young Men's Lyceum," 971; Lincoln, in *The Lincoln-Douglas Debates*, 199.

78 Saint Augustine, *Concerning the City of God against the Pagans*, trans. Henry Bettenson (London: Penguin Books, 1984), 877.

79 John Calvin, *Sermons on Titus*, trans. Robert White (Edinburgh: Banner of Truth, 2015), 228.

80 Calvin, *Sermons on Titus*, 227.

81 Calvin, *Sermons on Titus*, 226.

82 John Calvin, *Institutes of the Christian Religion*, vol. 2, trans. Ford Lewis Battles (Philadelphia: Westminster Press, 1960), 1503–504.

83 Thomas Aquinas, "Summa Theologica," in *Introduction to St. Thomas Aquinas*, ed. Anton C. Pegis (New York: Random House, 1948), 633.

84 Edmund Burke, *The Philosophy of Edmund Burke*, ed. Louis Bredvold and Ralph Ross (Ann Arbor: University of Michigan Press, 1960), 17.

85 Tertullian, "Apology," in *From Irenaeus to Grotius: A Sourcebook in Christian Political Thought*, ed. Oliver O'Donovan and Joan Lockwood O'Donovan (Grand Rapids and Cambridge, UK: William B. Eerdmans, 1999), 25.

86 Herndon and Weik, *Herndon's Lincoln*, 403.

87 Lincoln, "House Divided" Speech, 62.

88 David Herbert Donald, *"We Are Lincoln Men": Abraham Lincoln and His Friends"* (New York: Simon & Schuster, 2003), 47–48.

89 Woodworth, *While God Is Marching On*, 26.

90 Abraham Lincoln, "Second Inaugural Address," in *Classics of American Political and Constitutional Thought*, vol. 1, ed. Scott J. Hammond, Kevin R. Hardwick, and Howard L. Lubert (Indianapolis and Cambridge: Hackett Publishing Company, 2007), 1117.

Chapter 3

1 Donald, *"We Are Lincoln Men,"* 69–70.

2 William H. Herndon and Jesse W. Weik, *Herndon's Life of Lincoln*, ed. Paul M. Angle (Cleveland: World Publishing Company, 1930), 211.

3 Donald, *"We Are Lincoln Men,"* 76.

4 Herndon and Weik, *Herndon's Lincoln*, 60.

5 Herndon and Weik, *Herndon's Lincoln*, 328.

6 Lincoln, in *Herndon's Informants: Letters, Interviews, and Statements about Abraham Lincoln*, ed. Douglas L. Wilson and Rodney O. Davis (Urbana, IL: University of Illinois Press, 1998), 52–53.

7 Michael Burlingame, *The Black Man's President: Abraham Lincoln, African Americans, & the Pursuit of Racial Equality* (New York and London: Pegasus Books, 2021), 25.

8 Burlingame, *The Black Man's President*, 179.

9 Burlingame, *The Black Man's President*, 161.

10 Burlingame, *The Inner World of Abraham Lincoln*, 26.

11 Abraham Lincoln, "Gettysburg Address," in *Classics of American Political and Constitutional Thought*, vol. 1, ed. Scott J. Hammond, Kevin R. Hardwick, and Howard L. Lubert (Indianapolis and Cambridge: Hackett Publishing Company, 2007), 1113.

12 Abraham Lincoln, "First Inaugural Address," in *Classics of American Political and Constitutional Thought*, vol. 1, ed. Scott J. Hammond, Kevin R. Hardwick, and Howard L. Lubert (Indianapolis and Cambridge: Hackett Publishing Company, 2007), 1085.

13 Bertram Wyatt-Brown, "Church, Honor, and Secession," in *Religion and the American Civil War*, ed. Randall M. Miller, Harry S. Stout, and Charles Reagan Wilson (New York and Oxford: Oxford University Press, 1998), 89.

14 Sidney Blumenthal, *All the Powers of the Earth: The Political Life of Abraham Lincoln, Volume III, 1856–1860* (New York: Simon & Schuster, 2019), 628. Cf., McPherson, *For Cause and Comrades*, 14.

15 McPherson, *For Cause and Comrades*, 15.

16 Woodworth, *While God Is Marching On*, 290.

17 Charles Hodge, "The Princeton Review on the State of the Country and of the Church," *Biblical Repertory and Princeton Review* 37, no. 4 (1865): 639. Cf., McPherson, *For Cause and Comrades*, 19.

18 Harry Stout affirms, "Without the clergy's active endorsement of secession and war alongside that of the statesmen and generals, there could not have been a Confederate nation." *Upon the Altar of the Nation*, 43.

19 Thomas Cary Johnson, *The Life and Letters of Benjamin Morgan Palmer* (Richmond, VA: Presbyterian Committee of Publication, 1906), 209–10. Palmer's sermon was published in some fifty thousand pamphlets. Silver, *Confederate Morale and Church Propaganda*, 17.

20 Johnson, *The Life and Letters of Benjamin Morgan Palmer*, 210.

21 Dabney projected a different tone than Palmer on the prospect of war. Southerners, he maintained, should "weep tears of blood at the wretched and wicked thought" of war between North and South. Byrd, *A Holy Baptism of Fire and Blood*, 41.

22 Johnson, *The Life and Letters of Benjamin Morgan Palmer*, 213. James McPherson draws attention to the words of an Iowa volunteer who affirmed that the purpose of "this wicked rebellion" was "to secure the extension of that blighting curse—slavery—o'er our fair land." *For Cause and Comrades*, 19.

23 McPherson, *Abraham Lincoln*, 16.

24 Johnson, *The Life and Letters of Benjamin Morgan Palmer*, 216.

25 The area included in the Northwest Territory eventually became the states of Ohio, Indiana, Illinois, Michigan, and Wisconsin.

26 With respect to the new nation excluding slavery from the territories, Richard Carwardine states, "No other policy would have been consistent with the principles of natural rights, human equality, and political freedom laid out" in the "Declaration of Independence." *Lincoln: A Life of Purpose and Power*, 29.

27 Harold Holzer, *Lincoln at Cooper Union: The Speech That Made Abraham Lincoln President* (New York: Simon & Schuster, 2004), 113. Cf., Goodhart, "Lincoln and the Law," 53; Miller, *Lincoln's Virtues*, 10.

28 Abraham Lincoln, "Address at Cooper Institute," in *Lincoln Speeches*, ed. Allen C. Guelzo (New York: Penguin Books, 2012), 98–99.

29 Johnson, *The Life and Letters of Benjamin Morgan Palmer*, 216.

30 There was a sharp contrast between Charles Hodge and Palmer, two theologians of Old School Presbyterians. Palmer essentially predicted that Lincoln would become a tyrant. Hodge, on the other hand, voted for Lincoln and was overwhelmed with sorrow at his death. W. Andrew Hoffecker, *Charles Hodge: The Pride of Princeton* (Phillipsburg, NJ: P & R Publishing, 2011), 176, 420 note 10.

31 Johnson, *The Life and Letters of Benjamin Morgan Palmer*, 214. Reverend Thomas Smyth at Second Presbyterian Church in Charleston described Lincoln as an "unscrupulous and audacious tyrant" who "sanctions acts of military dictatorship which transcend the power of any monarch upon earth." Byrd, *A Holy Baptism of Fire and Blood*, 84.

32 *Recollected Words of Abraham Lincoln*, 5, provides a Lincoln quote from the *New York Post*. The president-elect explained why he did not respond to southern denunciations of his election: "I know the justness of my intentions and the utter groundlessness of the pretended fears of the men who are filling the country with their clamor."

33 Johnson, *The Life and Letters of Benjamin Morgan Palmer*, 217. Unlike Palmer, Robert L. Dabney who taught systematic theology at Union Theological Seminary maintained that the election of Lincoln was not a cause for secession. Silver, *Confederate Morale and Church Propaganda*, 20.

34 Hoffecker, *Charles Hodge: The Pride of Princeton*, 319.

35 Johnson, *The Life and Letters of Benjamin Morgan Palmer*, 215. The "invocation of the Founding Fathers" was a common theme. "Just as the American Patriots of 1776 had seceded from the tyrannical British empire, so the Southern Patriots of 1861 seceded from the tyrannical Yankee empire." McPherson, *For Cause and Comrades*, 21.

36 James Oscar Farmer, *The Metaphysical Confederacy: James Henley Thornwell and the Synthesis of Southern Values* (Macon, GA: Mercer University Press, 1986), 11. Stonewall Jackson spoke in similar terms. James I. Robertson, *Stonewall Jackson: the Man, the Soldier, the Legend* (New York: Macmillan Publishing, 1997), 234.

37 Johnson, *The Life and Letters of Benjamin Morgan Palmer*, 238. Cf., Silver, *Confederate Morale and Church Propaganda*, 14.

38 Johnson, *The Life and Letters of Benjamin Morgan Palmer*, 239.

39 Woodworth, *While God Is Marching On*, 94.

40 McPherson, *For Cause and Comrades*, 63, contends that the armies in the Civil War were "the most religious in American history." He further states, "There were few atheists in the rifle-pits of 1861–65."

41 Stout, *Upon the Altar of the Nation*, 49.

42 Stephen V. Ash, *When the Yankees Came: Conflict and Chaos in the Occupied South, 1861–1865* (Chapel Hill: University of North Carolina Press, 1995), 68–69.

43 Christopher H. Owen, *The Sacred Flame of Love: Methodism and Society in Nineteenth-Century Georgia* (Athens, GA: University of Georgia Press, 1998), 103–04. Cf., George M. Fredrickson, "The Coming of the Lord: The Northern Protestant Clergy and the Civil War Crisis," in *Religion and the American Civil War*, ed. Randall M. Miller, Harry S. Stout, and Charles Reagan Wilson (New York and Oxford: Oxford University Press, 1998), 118.

44 McPherson, *For Cause and Comrades*, 63, 75.

45 Nicholas Tyacke, "Puritanism, Arminianism, and Counter-Revolution," in *The Origins of the English Civil War*, ed. Conrad Russell (London: Macmillan, 1973), 143.

46 Johnson, *The Life and Letters of Benjamin Morgan Palmer*, 239.

47 Byrd, *A Holy Baptism of Fire and Blood*, 103.

48 John Morrill, *Oliver Cromwell* (Oxford: Oxford University Press, 2007), 60–62. Cf., Kurt O. Berends, "'Wholesome Reading Purifies and Elevates the Man': The Religious Military Press in the Confederacy," in *Religion and the American Civil War*, ed. Randall M. Miller, Harry S. Stout, and Charles Reagan Wilson (New York and Oxford: Oxford University Press, 1998), 142; Stout, *Upon the Altar of the Nation*, 80; Silver, *Confederate Morale and Church Propaganda*, 26.

49 Robertson, *Stonewall Jackson*, 234.

50 D. H. Dilbeck, "'The Sternest Feature of War': The Moral Dilemma of Retaliation and the Limits of Atrocity in the American Civil War," *Fides et Historia* 48, no. 1 (2016): 41.

51 George S. Burkhardt, *Confederate Rage, Yankee Wrath* (Carbondale, IL: Southern Illinois University Press, 2007), 1.

52 It should be noted, however, that two Union generals, William Tecumseh Sherman and Philip Sheridan, began in 1864 to order "life-for-life retaliation" in response to Confederate executions of white soldiers. Burkhardt, *Confederate Rage, Yankee Wrath*, 3.

53 Lincoln's "Letter to James C. Conkling," dated August 26, 1863, in *Lincoln's Speeches*, ed. Allen C. Guelzo (New York: Penguin Books, 2012), 147.

54 Lincoln was willing to call Stonewall Jackson "a brave, honest Presbyterian soldier." *Recollected Words of Abraham Lincoln*, 274.

55 John Calvin, *Commentaries on the Book of Joshua*, vol. 4 (Grand Rapids: Baker Book House, 1979), 268.

56 John Calvin, *Commentaries on the Last Four Books of Moses Arranged in the Form of a Harmony*, vol. 3 (Grand Rapids: Baker Book House, 1979), 52.

57 John Calvin, *Sermons on Deuteronomy* (Edinburgh: Banner of Truth, 1987), 734.

58 James Turner Johnson, *Just War Tradition and the Restraint of War: A Moral and Historical Inquiry* (Princeton: Princeton University Press, 1987), 137.

59 Eugene F. Rice and Anthony Grafton, *The Foundations of Early Modern Europe, 1460–1559*, 2d ed. (New York and London: W. W. Norton and Company, 1994), 137.

60 Steven Woodworth draws attention to Palmer's blessing upon Confederate troops at the beginning of the war, telling them that they were going to fight in a holy cause, "a war of religion." *While God Is Marching On*, 94, 137.

61 Woodworth, *While God Is Marching On*, 147.

62 George C. Rable, *God's Almost Chosen Peoples: A Religious History of the American Civil War* (Chapel Hill: University of North Carolina Press, 2010), 107.

63 Woodworth, *While God Is Marching On*, 158.

64 Woodworth, *While God Is Marching On*, 124.

65 Thomas Cary Johnson, *The Life and Letters of Robert Lewis Dabney* (Edinburgh: Banner of Truth, 1977), 239–40.

66 Johnson, *The Life and Letters of Robert Lewis Dabney*, 272.

67 Thomas Aquinas, *Summa Theologica*, vol. 3 (Allen, TX: Christian Classics, 1948), 1355.

68 Martin Luther, "On War against the Turk," in *Luther's Works*, ed. Jaroslav Pelikan, Helmut Lehman, and Robert Schultz, vol. 46 (St. Louis: Concordia Publishing House; Philadelphia: Fortress Press, 1967), 165.

69 Luther, "On War against the Turk," 168.

70 Luther, "On War against the Turk," 169.

71 Luther, "On War against the Turk," 180.

72 All citations from Zwingli's *Exposition of the Articles* appear in Huldrych Zwingli, *The Defense of the Reformed Faith*, trans. E. J. Furch (Allison Park, PA: Pickwick, 1984).

73 Article 41, in Zwingli, *Defense of the Reformed Faith*, 247.

74 Article 36, in Zwingli, *Defense of the Reformed Faith*, 250.

75 Oates, *Abraham Lincoln: The Man behind the Myths*, 80.

Chapter 4

1 Robert M. Kingdon, *Myths about the St. Bartholomew's Day Massacre, 1572–1576* (Cambridge, MA and London: Harvard University Press, 1988), 158.

2 Theodore Beza, *Concerning the Rights of Rulers over Their Subjects and the Duty of Subjects toward Their Rulers*, trans. Henry-Louis Gonin (Capetown and Pretoria: H.A.U.M., 1956), 44.

3 Beza, *Concerning the Rights of Rulers*, 31.

4 Beza, *Concerning the Rights of Rulers*, 30. In addition to the nation of Israel, Beza referred to the example of twelve additional states, beginning with Rome and concluding with France.

5 Beza, *Concerning the Rights of Rulers*, 27, 33–34, 45–60.

6 There was nothing illegal about the election of Lincoln to the presidency. Nevertheless, Reverend C. A. Davis of the Cumberland Presbyterian Church in Memphis maintained that there had been a usurpation of power resulting in the repeal of the Constitution. Silver, *Confederate Morale and Church Propaganda*, 32, note 38.

7 Lincoln, "Gettysburg Address," 1113.

8 John Calvin, Sermon 29, *Sermons on 1 Samuel*, trans. Douglas F. Kelly, in *Calvin Studies Colloquium* (Davidson, NC: Colloquium on Calvin Studies, 1982), 67.

9 John Calvin, *Commentaries on the Prophet Micah*, vol. 14 (Grand Rapids: Baker Book House, 1979), 309–10.

10 Calvin, *Institutes of the Christian Religion*, vol. 2, 1511.

11 Calvin, *Institutes of the Christian* Religion, vol. 2, 1512, 1516.

12 Calvin, *Institutes of the Christian* Religion, vol. 2, 1515.

13 At the Hampton Roads Peace Conference on February 3, 1865, Lincoln maintained that peace could only be restored if "those who were resisting the laws of the Union" would "cease that resistance." *Recollected Words of Abraham Lincoln*, 419–20.

14 Woodworth, *While God Is Marching On*, 95.

15 Calvin, *Institutes of the Christian* Religion, vol. 2, 1495.

16 John of Salisbury, "Policraticus," in *The Statesman's Book of John of Salisbury*, trans. John Dickinson (New York: Alfred A. Knopf, 1927), 258.

17 Ted Widmer, *Lincoln on the Verge: Thirteen Days to Washington* (New York: Simon & Schuster, 2020), 414, 418.

18 Widmer, *Lincoln on the Verge*, 415–19.

19 Thomas Aquinas, *On Kingship*, in *From Irenaeus to Grotius: A Sourcebook in Christian Political Thought*, ed. Oliver O'Donovan and Joan Lockwood O'Donovan (Grand Rapids and Cambridge, U.K.: William B. Eerdmans, 1999), 334.

20 Saint Augustine, "Reply to Faustus the Manichaean," in *The Nicene and Post-Nicene Fathers*, First Series, vol. 4 (Edinburgh: T & T Clark; Grand Rapids: William B. Eerdmans, 1996), 299.

21 Aquinas, *Summa Theologica*, vol. 3, 1354.

22 Robert E. Lee had taken the view that "secession is nothing less but revolution." He had affirmed that the Founders would not have "exhausted so much labor, wisdom, and forbearance" in framing the Constitution "if it was intended to be broken by every member of the Confederacy at will." Byrd, *A Holy Baptism of Fire and Blood*, 82.

23 Saint Augustine, *Concerning the City of God against the Pagans*, 866.

24 Four more states would secede after Lincoln called up 75,000 troops to put down the rebellion.

25 Harry V. Jaffa, *A New Birth of Freedom: Abraham Lincoln and the Coming of the Civil War* (Lanham, MD: Rowman & Littlefield, 2000), 358–59, provides this quotation from Lincoln's Message to Congress in Special Session, July 4, 1861.

26 Jaffa, *A New Birth of Freedom*, 359.

27 Even during his prairie years, Lincoln had developed a reputation as a peace-maker. Miller, *Lincoln's Virtues*, 32.

28 As a twenty-eight-year-old politician, Lincoln had made the same point in his "Protest Entered in the Illinois Legislature," 5, asserting that "the Congress of the United States has no power, under the constitution, to interfere with the institution of slavery in the different States." Cf., *Recollected Words of Abraham Lincoln,* 64–65, 421.

29 Lincoln, "First Inaugural Address," 1086.

30 Lincoln, "First Inaugural Address," 1087.

31 Lincoln, "First Inaugural Address," 1089. Goodhart states concerning Lincoln, "He did not believe that the southerners were wicked." "He believed that they were mistaken." "Lincoln and the Law," 71.

32 Abraham Lincoln, "Address to the Washington Temperance Society," in *Lincoln Speeches*, ed. Allen C. Guelzo (New York: Penguin Books, 2012), 20. Lincoln, "First Inaugural Address," 1086.

33 Oates, *Abraham Lincoln: The Man behind the Myths*, 83.

34 Jaffa, *A New Birth of Freedom*, 359.

35 Abraham Lincoln, "Speech at Independence Hall," in *Lincoln Speeches*, ed. Allen C. Guelzo (New York: Penguin Books, 2012), 111.

36 *Herndon's Informants*, 52.

37 Guelzo observes that Lincoln believed that the "republic" was "a nation, not merely a loose association based on 'self-interest.'" *Abraham Lincoln: Redeemer President*, 453–54.

38 Herman Belz, "Lincoln, Abraham (1809–65)," in *American Conservatism: An Encyclopedia*, ed. Bruce Frohnen, Jeremy Beer, and Jeffrey O. Nelson (Wilmington, DE: ISI Books, 2006), 517.

39 Maury Klein notes that the Constitution leaves "no clear trail" on the question of the legality of secession. Maury Klein, *Days of Defiance: Sumter, Secession, and the Coming of the Civil War* (New York: Alfred A. Knopff, 1997), 32–33.

40 Miller, *Lincoln's Virtues*, 114.

41 Oates, *Abraham Lincoln: The Man behind the Myths*, 48. Reverend Thomas Smyth took the view that secession was a "divine right." Silver, *Confederate Morale and Church Propaganda*, 51.

42 Oates, *Abraham Lincoln: The Man behind the* Myths, 5.

43 Guelzo, *Abraham Lincoln: Redeemer President*, 330.

44 Lincoln, "First Inaugural Address," 1086.

45 *Recollected Words of Abraham Lincoln*, 342.

46 Oates, *Abraham Lincoln: The Man behind the Myths*, 85.

47 Lincoln, "First Inaugural Address," 1089.

48 See Abraham Lincoln, "Speech on the War with Mexico," in *Lincoln Speeches*, ed. Allen C. Guelzo (New York: Penguin Books, 2012), 26, for a similar statement made on the floor of the United States House.

49 Lincoln, "First Inaugural Address," 1087.

50 Lincoln, "First Inaugural Address," 1087.

51 Lincoln, "First Inaugural Address," 1089.

52 McPherson, *Abraham Lincoln*, 31.

53 Phillip Shaw Paludan, "Religion and the American Civil War," in *Religion and the American Civil War*, ed. Randall M. Miller, Harry S. Stout, and Charles Reagan Wilson (New York and Oxford: Oxford University Press, 1998), 23, describes the firing on Fort Sumter as "a crisis in law and order." Cf., McPherson, *For Cause and Comrades*, 15, 18.

54 Ulysses S. Grant had the same view about the Mexican War. He asserted that it was "one of the most unjust ever waged by a stronger against a weaker nation." John Keegan, *The Mask of Command* (New York: Viking, 1987), 182.

55 Carwardine, *Lincoln: A Life of Purpose and Power*, 23.

56 Williams, *Lincoln and His Generals*, 315.

57 Jean-Jacques Burlamaqui, *The Principles of Natural and Political Law*, trans. Thomas Nugent (Indianapolis: Liberty Fund, 2006), 479.

58 Burlamaqui, *The Principles of Natural and Political Law*, 371–73.

59 Burlamaqui, *The Principles of Natural and Political Law*, 375.

60 The inferior magistrates in France would include the aristocrats and the rulers of cities who had been elected to office. Beza, *Concerning the Rights of Rulers*, 38–39.

61 Beza, *Concerning the Rights of Rulers*, 46.

62 Beza, *Concerning the Right of Rulers*, 48, 80. Johannes Althusius, the seventeenth-century jurist and Calvinist political philosopher, taught that tyranny occurs when the magistrate "violates, changes, or overthrows the fundamental laws of the realm." Johannes Althusius, *Politica*, trans. Frederick S. Carney (Indianapolis: Liberty Fund, 1995), 192.

63 Lincoln, "First Inaugural Address," 1085.

64 Rable, *God's Almost Chosen Peoples*, 57, observes that Charles Hodge "denied that the supposed grievances of the southern states could justify rebellion."Aquinas, *Summa Theologica*, vol. 3, 1359.

65 Beza, *Concerning the Rights of Rulers*, 73–74.

66 Carwardine, *Lincoln: A Life of Purpose and Power*, 169. Cf., Rable, *God's Almost Chosen Peoples*, 52.

67 Aquinas, *Summa Theologica*, vol. 3, 1359.

68 Calvin, *Institutes of the Christian Religion*, vol. 2, 1511.

69 *Recollected Words of Abraham Lincoln*, 336–37.

70 Robertson, *Stonewall Jackson*, 213.

71 Herndon and Weik, *Herndon's Lincoln*, 329, 331. Cf., McPherson, *For Cause and Comrades*, 16–17; Keegan, *The Mask of Command*, 189.

72 Goodhart, "Lincoln and the Law," 68.

73 Goodhart, "Lincoln and the Law," 68.

74 "The Constitution of the United States of America," in *The American Republic: Primary Sources*, ed. Bruce Frohnen (Indianapolis: Liberty Fund, 2002), 236.

75 Guelzo, *Abraham Lincoln: Redeemer President*, 283. McPherson observes, "At issue was not whether the writ could be suspended, but *who* could suspend it." *Abraham Lincoln*, 43.

76 *Inside Lincoln's White House: The Complete Civil War Diary of John Hay*, ed. Michael Burlingame and John R. Turner Ettlinger (Carbondale, IL: Southern Illinois University Press, 1997), 20.

Chapter 5

1 Hopkins, "A Dialogue Concerning the Slavery of the Africans," 156.

2 Lincoln, "Second Inaugural Address," 1117–118.

3 Jonathan Edwards, "A Strong Rod Broken and Withered," in *The Works of Jonathan Edwards*, vol. 25, ed. Wilson H. Kimnach (New Haven: Yale University Press, 2006), 316.

4 Edwards, "A Strong Rod Broken and Withered," 330.

5 Iain H. Murray, *Jonathan Edwards: A New Biography* (Edinburgh: Banner of Truth, 1987), 286–87. Cf., Jeff Jay Stone, "The Political Philosophy of Jonathan Edwards" (Ph.D. diss., University of Dallas, 1992), 12.

6 Edwards, "A Strong Rod Broken and Withered," 321.

7 Augustine of Hippo had asserted the same position in the early fifth century in his classic work the *City of God*, 170.

8 Jonathan Edwards Jr., "The Necessity of the Belief of Christianity," in *Political Sermons of the Founding Era, 1730–1805*, ed. Ellis Sandoz (Indianapolis: Liberty Press), 1189. Edwards preached this message before the Connecticut General Assembly on May 8, 1794.

9 Edwards Jr., "The Necessity of the Belief of Christianity," 1191.

10 Edwards Jr., "The Necessity of the Belief of Christianity," 1189.

11 Edwards Jr., "The Necessity of the Belief of Christianity," 1195.

12 Edwards Jr., "The Necessity of the Belief of Christianity," 1196.

13 Edwards Jr., "The Necessity of the Belief of Christianity," 1199.

14 Edwards Jr., "The Necessity of the Belief of Christianity," 1202–206.

15 James H. Thornwell, "Relation of the State to Christ," in *The Collected Writings of James Henley* Thornwell, vol. 4 (Edinburgh: Banner of Truth, 1974), 551.

16 Thornwell, "Sermon on National Sins," 546.

17 Joseph J. Ellis, *Founding Brothers: The Revolutionary Generation* (New York: Alfred A. Knopf, 2000), 120.

18 Thornwell, "Sermon on National Sins," 546.

19 Palmer, *The Life and Letters of James Henley Thornwell*, 287.

20 James H. Moorhead, *American Apocalypse: Yankee Protestants and the Civil War, 1860–1869* (New Haven and London: Yale University Press, 1978), x.

21 Thornwell, "Sermon on National Sins," 529.

22 Thornwell, "Sermon on National Sins," 523.

23 Palmer, *The Life and Letters of James Henley Thornwell*, 342.

24 Daniel Walker Howe, *The Political Culture of the American Whigs* (Chicago and London: University of Chicago Press, 1979), 25.

25 Thornwell, "Sermon on National Sins," 535.

26 Thornwell, "Sermon on National Sins," 525.

27 Robert L. Dabney, "Christians, Pray for Your Country," in *Discussions: Evangelical and Theological*, vol. 2 (Edinburgh: Banner of Truth, 1967), 397.

28 Dabney rejected the classical contract theories that traced the origin of government to a merely human origin. *Systematic Theology* (Edinburg: Banner of Truth, 1985), 863.

29 Robert L. Dabney, "The Christian Soldier," in *Discussions: Evangelical and Theological*, vol. 1 (Edinburgh: Banner of Truth, 1967), 614.

30 Dabney, *Systematic Theology*, 863.

31 Thomas Cary Johnson, *The Life and Letters of Robert Lewis Dabney* (Edinburgh: Banner of Truth, 1977), 307.

32 Dabney, "Christians, Pray for Your Country," 393.

33 Gordon S. Wood, *Empire of Liberty: A History of the Early Republic, 1789–1815* (Oxford and New York: Oxford University Press, 2009), 583, notes that five of the original state constitutions—New Hampshire, Connecticut, New Jersey, North Carolina, and Georgia—required officeholders to be Protestant.

34 Robert L. Dabney, "Civic Ethics," in *Discussions: Evangelical and Theological*, vol. 3 (Edinburgh: Banner of Truth, 1967), 120.

35 Dabney, "Christians, Pray for Your Country," 399.

36 Robert L. Dabney, "The Christian's Best Motive for Patriotism," in *Discussions: Evangelical and Theological*, vol. 2 (Edinburgh: Banner of Truth, 1974), 409.

37 Forrest McDonald, *Novus Ordo Seclorum: The Intellectual Origins of the Constitution* (Lawrence, KS: University Press of Kansas, 1985), 70–71.

38 Dabney, "Christians, Pray for Your Country," 397–98.

39 Bertram Wyatt-Brown, *Southern Honor: Ethics and Behavior in the Old South* (New York and Oxford: Oxford University Press, 1982), 107.

40 Dabney, "The Christian's Best Motive for Patriotism," 407.

41 Dabney, "The Christian's Best Motive for Patriotism," 407.

42 Clement Eaton, *The Growth of Southern Civilization, 1790–1860* (New York: Harper and Brothers, 1961), 275; Steven J. Keilor, *This Rebellious House: American History and the Truth of Christianity* (Downers Grove, IL: Intervarsity Press, 1996), 127–49.

43 John H. Franklin, *The Militant South, 1800–1861* (Cambridge: Harvard University Press, 1956), 35.

44 Dabney, "The Christian's Best Motive for Patriotism," 407.

45 *Recollected Words of Abraham Lincoln*, 299.

46 Wills, *Lincoln at Gettysburg*, 179.

Chapter 6

1 Douglas L. Wilson and Rodney O. Davis, *Herndon's Informants: Letters, Interviews, and Statements about Abraham Lincoln* (Urbana: University of Illinois Press, 1998), 394.

2 Lincoln's compassion is reflected on by James Speed, in *An Oral History of Abraham* Lincoln, ed. Michael Burlingame (Carbondale, IL: Southern Illinois Press, 1996), 80–82.

3 *Herndon's Informants*, 214.

4 *Herndon's Informants*, 107–08.

5 Miller, *Lincoln's Virtues*, 28.

6 Lincoln wrote a letter to Speed, dated August 24, 1855, in which he concluded with the words "Your friend forever A. Lincoln." *Herndon's Informants*, 55.

7 *Herndon's Informants*, 590. Matilda Johnston, Lincoln's stepsister, said, "Abe preached against Cruelty to animals, Contending that an ants life was to it, as sweet as ours to us." *Herndon's Informants*, 109.

8 Wills, *Lincoln at Gettysburg*, 171, provides a humorous quote from Lincoln regarding the Second Inaugural and the fact that it contained only six hundred words. Lincoln said, "Lots of wisdom in that document, I suspect."

9 Goodhart, "Lincoln and the Law," 56.

10 Herndon and Weik, *Herndon's Lincoln*, 320.

11 Herndon and Weik, *Herndon's Lincoln*, 321.

12 *Herndon's Informants*, 350.

13 Ronald C. White, *A Lincoln: A Biography* (New York: Random House, 2009), 668. Cf., *Inside Lincoln's White House*, 64.

14 Miller, *Lincoln's Virtues*, 11.

15 Michael Burlingame, *Abraham Lincoln: A Life*, vol. 1 (Baltimore: Johns Hopkins University Press, 2008), 361.

16 Herndon and Weik, *Herndon's Lincoln*, 18, 41; Guelzo, *Abraham Lincoln as a Man of Ideas*, 18–20, surveys the wide-array of intellectual interests of Lincoln. Lincoln told his friend Noah Brooks, a reporter for the *Daily Union* of Sacramento, California, that he "always hoped to get at Edwards on the will."

17 *Herndon's* Informants, 114; Cf., Doris Kearns Goodwin, *Team of Rivals: The Political Genius of Abraham Lincoln* (New York: Simon & Schuster, 2006), 49.

18 *Herndon's Informants*, 499.

19 Richard Striner, *Summoned to Glory: The Audacious Life of Abraham Lincoln* (Lanham, MD: Rowman & Littlefield, 2020), 9.

20 Miller, *Lincoln's Virtues*, 37.

21 Douglas L. Wilson, *Honor's Voice: The Transformation of Abraham Lincoln* (New York: Alfred A. Knopf, 1998), 76–85; *Herndon's Informants*, 432, 529; Carwardine, *Lincoln's Sense of Humor*, 9.

22 White, *A Lincoln*, 55; Blumenthal, *A Self-Made Man*, 604–08.

23 Guelzo, *Abraham Lincoln as a Man of Ideas*, 18.

24 Herndon and Weik, *Herndon's Lincoln*, 266.

25 Lincoln later defeated Cartwright in the election for the United State House in 1846.

26 Guelzo, *Abraham Lincoln: Redeemer President*, 51.

27 David S. Reynolds, *Abe: Abraham Lincoln in His Times* (New York: Penguin Books, 2020), 110.

28 Joshua Speed, *Herndon's Informants*, 431, referred to Lincoln's "early love for Miss Rutledge."

29 *Herndon's Informants*, 604–05.

30 *Herndon's Informants*, 21.

31 Herndon and Weik, *Herndon's Lincoln*, 90.

32 Herndon and Weik, *Herndon's Lincoln*, 94.

33 Lincoln later married Mary Todd, but Judge David Davis maintained that Lincoln was "not domestically happy." He stated, "As a general rule when all the lawyers of a Saturday Evening would go home and see their families & friends at home Lincoln would refuse to go home." *Herndon's Informants*, 349.

34 Carl Sandburg, *Abraham Lincoln: The Prairie Years*, vol. 1 (New York: Charles Scribner's Sons, 1944), 189–90.

35 *Herndon's Informants*, 236.

36 Herndon and Weik, *Herndon's Lincoln*, 95.

37 *Recollected Words of Abraham Lincoln*, 296.

38 Carwardine, *Lincoln: A Life of Purpose and Power*, 36.

39 McPherson, *Abraham Lincoln*, 8.

40 Miller, *Lincoln's Virtues*, 7.

41 Herndon and Weik, *Herndon's Lincoln*, 266; Cf., *Herndon's Informants*, 519, 529, 576.

42 *An Oral History of Abraham Lincoln*, 14.

43 *An Oral History of Abraham Lincoln*, ed. Michael Burlingame (Carbondale, IL: Southern Illinois Press, 1996), 131.

44 *An Oral History of Abraham Lincoln*, 5. Niebuhr concludes that "Lincoln's religious convictions were superior in depth and purity to those" of "the religious leaders of the era." Reinhold Niebuhr, "The Religion of Abraham Lincoln," in *Lincoln and the Gettysburg Address*, ed. Allan Nevins (Urbana: University of Illinois Press, 1964), 72–73.

45 Benjamin P. Thomas, *Abraham Lincoln: A Biography* (New York: Barnes & Noble Books, 1952), 68.

46 Mary Todd Lincoln drew a connection between her husband's sorrows and his turning to the Lord. Herndon and Weik, *Herndon's Lincoln*, 269.

47 Burlingame, *Abraham Lincoln*, vol. 1, 25.

48 Herndon and Weik, *Herndon's Lincoln*, 351.

49 The death of Eddie in 1850 appears to have been a turning point in Lincoln's life, for "there is no evidence through the 1840s that Lincoln attended any church in Springfield." Guelzo, *Abraham Lincoln as a Man of Ideas*, 18.

50 Woodworth, *While God Is Marching On*, 24.

51 Ronald C. White, *Lincoln's Greatest Speech: The Second Inaugural* (New York: Simon & Schuster, 2002), 130.

52 Mary Lincoln stated that her husband's heart was "directed towards religion" following the death of Eddie. Burlingame, *Abraham Lincoln*, vol. 1, 359.

53 White, *Lincoln in Private*, 113.

54 Carwardine, *Lincoln: A Life of Purpose and Power*, 37.

55 *Recollected Words of Abraham Lincoln*, 296.

56 Carwardine affirms, "The mature Lincoln of the 1850s was more receptive to Protestant orthodoxy than he had been twenty years earlier." *Lincoln: A Life of Purpose and Power*, 34.

57 Sidney Blumenthal provides no evidence for his characterization of Lincoln's letter to his dying father. He affirms it was "falsely sentimental" and that Lincoln did not believe that heaven existed. Sidney Blumenthal, *Wrestling with His Angel: The Political Life of Abraham Lincoln, Volume II, 1849–1856* (New York: Simon & Schuster, 2017), 133. Joshua Zeitz, *Lincoln's God: How Faith Transformed a President and a Nation* (New York: Viking, 2023), 21, likewise reflects an unwarranted skepticism.

58 Herndon and Weik, *Herndon's Lincoln*, 21.

59 *Herndon's Informants*, 156.

60 *Herndon's Informants*, 497. Cf., *Recollected Words of Abraham Lincoln*, 345.

61 Reynolds, *Abe*, 628.

62 Herndon and Weik, *Herndon's Lincoln*, 315.

63 Michael Burlingame, *Abraham Lincoln: A Life*, vol. 2 (Baltimore: Johns Hopkins University Press, 2008), 819.

64 David Herbert Donald observes concerning Lincoln, "After he began to feel the burdens of the presidency, he frequently asked for God's aid." David Herbert Donald, *Lincoln* (New York: Simon & Schuster, 1995), 337.

65 Guelzo, *Abraham Lincoln: Redeemer President*, 321.

66 Burlingame, *Abraham* Lincoln, vol. 2, 256. Cf., Carwardine, *Lincoln: A Life of Purpose and Power*, 34.

67 Burlingame, *Abraham Lincoln*, vol. 2, 298.

68 White, *A. Lincoln*, 476–77.

69 White, *A. Lincoln*, 627.

70 *An Oral History of Abraham Lincoln*, 131.

71 Blumenthal, *Wrestling with His Angel*, 209, is an example of this.

72 Woodworth, *While God Is Marching On*, 36.

73 *Recollected Words of Abraham Lincoln*, 437.

74 Guelzo refers to Lincoln's "ancestral Calvinism" which "reappeared as a device for interpreting the events of the Civil War." *Abraham Lincoln as a Man of Ideas*, 20.

75 White, *A. Lincoln*, 622.

76 Guelzo, *Abraham Lincoln as a Man of Ideas*, 24.

77 White, *A. Lincoln*, 627.

78 White, *A. Lincoln*, 622.

79 Noll is willing to say that Lincoln went beyond the theologians of his time: "None penetrated as deeply into the nature of providence." *America's God*, 426.

80 Noll observes, "For Lincoln there was awesome mystery" in "how God dealt with the world." *America's God*, 435.

81 White, *A. Lincoln*, 622.

82 Richard Brookhiser, *Founders' Son: A Life of Abraham Lincoln* (New York: Basic Books, 2014), 280. Cf., Noll, *The Civil War as a Theological Crisis*, 87–88.

83 Lincoln, "Second Inaugural Address," 1117.

Chapter 7

1 *Recollected Words of Abraham Lincoln*, 511.

2 Abraham Lincoln, "Speech to the One Hundred Sixty-Six Ohio Regiment," in *Lincoln Speeches*, ed. Allen C. Guelzo (New York: Penguin Books, 2012), 153.

3 Herndon and Weik, *Herndon's Lincoln*, 39.

4 Herndon and Weik, *Herndon's Lincoln*, 15. Lincoln did not remain in poverty. When Lincoln married he was earning $1,200 a year, an income equal to the salary of the governor. His annual income eventually reached $5,000. McPherson, *Abraham Lincoln*, 12, 14–15.

5 *Recollected Words of Abraham Lincoln*, 330.

6 Guelzo reflects upon the subsistence-farming family into which Lincoln was born and the fact that he disliked farmwork. "He disliked the uncouthness, violence, and drunkenness of his neighbors." *Abraham Lincoln as a Man of Ideas*, 17.

7 *Recollected Words of Abraham Lincoln*, 508.

8 Thomas, *Abraham Lincoln*, 14; Miller, *Lincoln's Virtues*, 22.

9 *Herndon's Informants*, 111.

10 Herndon and Weik, *Herndon's Lincoln*, 30.

11 Thomas, *Abraham Lincoln*, 9; Cf., *Herndon's Informants*, 28.

12 Herndon and Weik, *Herndon's Lincoln*, 28; *Herndon's Informants*, 40; Oates, *Abraham Lincoln: The Man behind the Myths*, 36; Miller, *Lincoln's Virtues*, 47, points out that nine people lived in the small cabin.

13 Guelzo, *Abraham Lincoln: Redeemer President*, 31.

14 Thomas, *Abraham Lincoln*, 9.

15 Herndon and Weik, *Herndon's Lincoln*, 35.

16 Guelzo, *Abraham Lincoln: Redeemer President*, 32–33.

17 The Sangamon River empties into the Illinois River, which connects with the Mississippi just north of Alton, Illinois.

18 Herndon and Weik, *Herndon's Lincoln*, 55.

19 Herndon and Weik, *Herndon's Lincoln*, 347.

20 Herndon and Weik, *Herndon's Lincoln*, 298–99.

21 Herndon and Weik, *Herndon's Lincoln*, 310.

22 *Herndon's Informants*, 590.

23 Burlingame, *The Black Man's President*, 178.

24 Burlingame, *The Inner World of Abraham Lincoln*, 13.

25 Abraham Lincoln, "Eulogy on Henry Clay," in *Lincoln Speeches*, ed. Allen C. Guelzo (New York: Penguin Books, 2012), 37.

26 *Recollected Words of Abraham Lincoln*, 31.

27 *An Oral History of Abraham Lincoln*, 131.

28 *Recollected Words of Abraham Lincoln*, 330–31.

29 John Calvin, *Commentary on the Book of Psalms*, vol. 4 (Grand Rapids: Baker Book House, 1979), xl.

30 Calvin, *Institutes of the Christian Religion*, vol. 2, 1513.

31 John Calvin, *Commentaries on the Epistle to the Romans*, vol. 19 (Grand Rapids: Baker Book House, 1979), 478.

32 Lincoln identified himself not so much as being "a Northern man," but "rather, a Western free state man." "Speech on the 1848 Presidential Race," in *Lincoln Speeches*, ed. Allen C. Guelzo (New York: Penguin Books, 2012), 28. Cf., Carwardine, *Lincoln's Sense of Humor*, 94.

33 White, *Lincoln's Greatest Speech*, 131–32.

34 Lincoln was attracted to intellectual preaching. Burlingame points out that he was impressed after listening to a sermon coming from the "productive" mind of Henry Ward Beecher. *Abraham Lincoln*, vol. 2, 591.

35 Donald, *Lincoln*, 337, 599. Guelzo, *Abraham Lincoln: Redeemer President*, 437–38.

36 Guelzo, *Abraham Lincoln: Redeemer President*, 453.

37 Oates, *Abraham Lincoln: The Man behind the Myths*, 53–54.

38 John Wesley Hill, *Abraham Lincoln, Man of God* (New York and London: G. P. Putnam's Sons, 1920), 239.

39 Hill, *Abraham Lincoln, Man of God*, 239.

40 Widmer, *Lincoln on the Verge*, 452.

41 Widmer, *Lincoln on the Verge*, 120.

42 Lincoln, "First Inaugural Address," 1089.

43 Brookhiser puts it this way: "He had faced God the Father directly. He wrestled with Him" as "Jacob had wrestled with the angel." *Founders' Son*, 284.

44 This was the testimony of Orville Browning, *An Oral History of Abraham Lincoln*, 130.

45 Lincoln visited Farmington, the Speed plantation near Louisville, in 1841. Lucy Speed, Joshua's mother, was "much pained at his [Lincoln's] depression." She "presented him a bible—advising him to read it—to adopt its precepts and pray for its promises." "It made a deep impression upon him." *Herndon's Informants*, 342.

46 Reverend James Smith who provided pastoral care for the Lincolns following the death of Eddie stated, "Mr. Lincoln did avow his belief in the Divine Authority and Inspiration [of] the Scriptures." Guelzo, *Abraham Lincoln: Redeemer President*, 444.

47 Unlike Speed, Lincoln stood in continuity with John Locke, "Infallibility," in *Writings on Religion*, ed. Victor Nuovo (Oxford: Clarendon Press, 2002), 71. "Holy Scripture," said Locke, "contains within it profound mysteries of divine things that absolutely surpass human understanding." "Their "truth is certain and to be believed, but how they are such" cannot be "conceived in the mind."

48 Donald, *"We Are Lincoln Men,"* 63; *Recollected Words of Abraham Lincoln*, 414.

49 Reynolds, *Abe*, 37.

50 Burlingame, *Abraham Lincoln*, vol. 1, 38. Cf., Passos, "Lincoln and His Almost Chosen People," 24.

51 *Herndon's Informants*, 521.

52 *An Oral History of Abraham Lincoln*, 130. Cf., *Recollected Words of Abraham Lincoln*, 362.

53 Herndon and Weik, *Herndon's Lincoln*, 372.

54 *Herndon's Informants*, 40.

55 Herndon and Weik, *Herndon's Lincoln*, 22.

56 *Herndon's Informants*, 113.

57 Herndon and Weik, *Herndon's Lincoln*, 16.

58 Burlingame, *Abraham Lincoln*, vol. 1, 19.

59 Herndon and Weik, *Herndon's Lincoln*, 30–31; *Herndon's Informants*, 40.

60 *Herndon's Informants*, 94. The original spelling has been retained.

61 *Herndon's Informants*, 40; Blumenthal, *A Self-Made Man*, 26.

62 White, *A. Lincoln*, 18.

63 Reynolds, *Abe*, 36; *Herndon's Informants*, 615.

64 Herndon and Weik, *Herndon's Lincoln*, 31, 46, 56–57.

65 McPherson, *Abraham Lincoln*, 46.

66 Williams, *Lincoln and His Generals*, 36.

67 McPherson, *Abraham Lincoln*, 56–57.

68 The platform of 1864 went beyond the Republican Party platform of 1860 which conceded "the right of each state to order and control its own domestic institutions according to its own judgment exclusively."

69 The Thirteenth Amendment was passed by Congress on January 31, 1865, and ratified on December 6, 1865.

70 Moorhead, *American Apocalypse*, 176.

71 McPherson, *Abraham Lincoln*, 61.

Chapter 8

1 *Herndon's Informants*, 41.

2 Herndon wrote about the way that Lincoln bade farewell to him following his visit to Washington in the late summer of 1861. He stated, "I separated from Mr. Lincoln at the White House. He followed me to the near portico." "He grasped me warmly by the hand and bade me a fervent 'Good-bye.' It was the last time I ever saw him alive." Herndon and Weik, *Herndon's Lincoln*, 304.

3 Herndon and Weik, *Herndon's Lincoln*, 33; *Herndon's Informants*, 108.

4 Oates, *Abraham Lincoln: The Man behind the Myths*, 45–47; *Recollected Words of Abraham Lincoln*, 503.

5 Striner, *Summoned to Glory: The Audacious Life of Abraham Lincoln*, 448.

6 *Recollected Words of Abraham Lincoln*, 398.

7 Elizabeth Keckley indicated that Lincoln on the day of his assassination, while looking at a picture of Lee said, "It is a good face; it is the face of a noble, noble, brave man. I am glad that the war is over at last." *Recollected Words of Abraham Lincoln*, 275.

8 J. David Hacker, "A Census-Based Count of the Civil War Dead," 57, no. 4 (December 2011): 306–47.

9 Stephen E. Ambrose, *To America: Personal Reflections of an Historian* (New York: Simon & Schuster, 2002), 60–61.

10 *Recollected Words of Abraham Lincoln*, 365.

11 Silver, *Confederate Morale and Church Propaganda*, 88.

12 *Recollected Words of Abraham Lincoln*, 182.

13 *Recollected Words of Abraham Lincoln*, 404.

14 *Recollected Words of Abraham Lincoln*, 435.

15 *Recollected Words of Abraham Lincoln*, 143.

16 *Recollected Words of Abraham Lincoln*, 339.

17 Striner, *Summoned to Glory: The Audacious Life of Abraham Lincoln*, 459.

18 Martin Luther, "Against the Robbing and Murdering Hordes of Peasants," in *Luther's Works*, vol. 46, ed. Jaroslav Pelikan, Helmut T. Lehman, and Robert C. Schultz (St. Louis: Concordia Publishing House; Philadelphia: Fortress Press, 1967), 50.

19 Luther, "Against the Robbing and Murdering Hordes of Peasants," 53.

20 Byrd, *A Holy Baptism of Fire and Blood*, 261.

21 Guelzo, *Abraham Lincoln: Redeemer President*, 449.

22 Oates, *Abraham Lincoln: The Man behind the Myths*, 166. Cf., McPherson, *Abraham Lincoln*, 61; *Inside Lincoln's White House*, 188.

23 Burlingame, *Abraham Lincoln*, vol. 2, 799.

24 *Recollected Words of Abraham Lincoln*, 428.

25 Oates, *Abraham Lincoln: The Man behind the Myths*, 89.

26 John Todd Stuart affirmed that he visited Lincoln in Washington "not more than a week before he died." Lincoln told him that it was his desire to return to Springfield to live out the remainder of his days "after his time as President was out." *An Oral History of Abraham Lincoln*, 14.

27 Herndon and Weik, *Herndon's Lincoln*, 290; *Recollected Words of American Lincoln*, 397.

28 Herndon and Weik, *Herndon's Lincoln*, 264.

29 Edward Achorn, *Every Drop of Blood: The Momentous Second Inauguration of Abraham Lincoln* (New York: Atlantic Monthly Press, 2020), 160–65.

30 *Recollected Words of Abraham Lincoln*, 45.

31 *Recollected Words of Abraham Lincoln*, 349.

32 *Recollected Words of Abraham Lincoln*, 355.

33 Herndon and Weik, *Herndon's Lincoln*, 338.

34 Williams, *Lincoln and His Generals*, 326.

35 *Recollected Words of Abraham Lincoln*, 383.

36 *Recollected Words of Abraham Lincoln*, 384–85.

37 *Recollected Words of Abraham Lincoln*, 339–40; Carwardine, *Lincoln: A Life of Purpose and Power*, 316.

38 Calvin, *Institutes of the Christian Religion*, vol. 1, 40.

39 Calvin, *Institutes of the Christian Religion*, vol. 1, 40–41.

40 Calvin, *Institutes of the Christian Religion*, vol. 1, 41.

41 Calvin, *Institutes of the Christian Religion*, vol. 1, 341.

42 Calvin, *Institutes of the Christian Religion*, vol. 1, 537.

43 Calvin, *Institutes of the Christian Religion*, vol. 1, 565.

44 Herndon and Weik, *Herndon's Lincoln*, 21.

45 *Recollected Words of Abraham Lincoln*, 25.

46 White, *Lincoln's Greatest Speech*, 139.

47 Carwardine, *Lincoln: A Life of Purpose and Power*, 37.

48 Herndon and Weik, *Herndon's Lincoln*, 322.

49 Burlingame, *Abraham Lincoln*, vol. 2, 820. Grant also was thoroughly convinced that the cause of the North was just. His *Memoirs* were intended to explain "how a just triumphed over an unjust cause." Keegan, *The Mask of Command*, 202.

50 Noll, *America's God*, 426.

51 Charles Hodge, "President Lincoln," *Biblical Repertory and Princeton Review* 37, no. 3 (1865): 435.

52 McPherson, *For Cause and Comrades*, 118.

53 Snay, *Gospel of Disunion*, 78.

54 Bradley J. Gundlach, "'Wicked Caste': Warfield, Biblical Authority, and Jim Crow," in *B. B. Warfield: Essays on His Life and Thought*, ed. Gary L. W. Johnson (Phillipsburg, NJ: P&R Publishing, 2007), 142. Lincoln and his wife Mary Todd heard Breckinridge preach at Second Presbyterian Church in Lexington, Kentucky, on November 25, 1847.

55 Hodge, "President Lincoln," 439–40. Cf., Eugene D. Genovese, "Religion in the Collapse of the American Union," in *Religion and the American Civil War*, Randall M. Miller, Harry S. Stout, and Charles Reagan Wilson (New York and Oxford: Oxford University Press, 1998), 87, note 28.

56 *Herndon's Informants*, 197.

57 McPherson, *For Cause and Comrades*, 19. There were, of course, many soldiers who enlisted only to preserve the Union (122–23).

58 Woodworth, *While God Is Marching On*, 292–94.

59 John Calvin, *Sermons on the Epistle to the Ephesians* (Edinburgh: Banner of Truth, 1973), 642.

60 Calvin, *Sermons on the Epistle to the Ephesians*, 634.

61 Donald observes that Lincoln's best friend, Joshua Speed, "had no moral repugnance to owning slaves." He bought slaves "so that by 1850 he had eighteen." *"We Are Lincoln Men,"* 54.

62 John Calvin, *Commentaries on the Book of the Prophet Jeremiah and the Lamentations*, vol. 10 (Grand Rapids: Baker Book House, 1979), 283.

63 Carwardine, *Lincoln's Sense of Humor*, 73.

64 John Calvin, *Commentaries on the First Book of Moses Called Genesis*, vol. 1 (Grand Rapids: Baker Book House, 1979), 351.

65 Calvin, *Sermons on the Epistle to the Ephesians*, 633.

66 Calvin, *Commentaries on the Book of the Prophet Jeremiah and the Lamentations*, vol. 10, 284.

67 *Recollected Words of Abraham Lincoln*, 183.

68 *Herndon's Informants*, 348.

69 It should be noted that Stephens had maintained on November 14, 1860, in a speech before the Georgia legislature that secession violated the Constitution. Byrd, *A Holy Baptism of Fire and Blood*, 44–45.

70 Alexander Stephens, "Cornerstone Speech," in *Classics of American Political and Constitutional Thought*, vol. 1, ed. Scott J. Hammond, Kevin R. Hardwick, and Howard L. Lubert (Indianapolis and Cambridge: Hackett Publishing Company, 2007), 1092.

71 Stephens, "Cornerstone Speech," 1091.

72 Stephens, "Cornerstone Speech," 1092.

73 McPherson draws attention to Northern soldiers commenting on the cruelty and inhumanity of the slave system which allowed a master to whip a slave as he pleased. *For Cause and Comrades*, 118.

74 Burlingame, *The Black Man's President*, 15.

75 Calvin, *Commentaries on the First Book of Moses Called Genesis*, vol. 1, 351.

76 Reverend Joseph Ruggles Wilson, pastor of First Presbyterian Church in Augusta, Georgia, believed—contrary to Augustine—that slavery was "so central to God's designs that it would persist into the millennium." Stout, *Upon the Altar of the Nation*, 43–44.

77 Saint Augustine, *Concerning the City of God against the Pagans*, 874.

78 Saint Augustine, *Concerning the City of God against the Pagans*, 875.

79 Saint Augustine, *Concerning the City of God against the Pagans*, 858.

80 Saint Augustine, *Concerning the City of God against the Pagans*, 859–60.

81 Saint Augustine, *Concerning the City of God against the Pagans*, 861.

82 Saint Augustine, *Concerning the City of God against the Pagans*, 862.

83 *Recollected Words of Abraham Lincoln*, 388.

84 Lincoln, "Gettysburg Address," 1113.

85 Lincoln, "Second Inaugural Address," 1118.

86 Saint Augustine, *Concerning the City of God against the Pagans*, 857.

87 Burlingame, *Abraham Lincoln*, vol. 1, 25.

88 Hebrews 11:16.

89 Herndon and Weik, *Herndon's Lincoln*, 21.

90 Carwardine, *Lincoln: A Life of Purpose and Power*, 315.

91 Saint Augustine, *Concerning the City of God against the Pagans*, 865.

92 *Recollected Words of Abraham* Lincoln, 297; Guelzo, *Abraham Lincoln: Redeemer President*, 434.

93 Saint Augustine, *Concerning the City of God against the Pagans*, 875.

94 Saint Augustine, *Concerning the City of God against the Pagans*, 1088.

Conclusion

1 Herndon and Weik, *Herndon's Lincoln*, 55.

2 *Recollected Words of Abraham Lincoln*, 388.

3 Williams, *Lincoln and His Generals*, vii, 7.

4 Hill, *Abraham Lincoln, Man of God*, 239.

5 Herndon and Weik, *Herndon's Lincoln*, 357.

6 White, *Lincoln in Private*, 25.

7 *Herndon's Informants*, 590.

8 *Recollected Words of Abraham Lincoln*, 330–31.

9 *Recollected Words of Abraham Lincoln*, 365.

10 Lincoln, *The Lincoln-Douglas Debates*, 271.

11 "The Declaration of Independence," 189.

12 Calvin, *Institutes of the Christian Religion*, vol. 2, 1503–504.

13 Martin Luther, *Commentary on Romans*, trans. J. Theodore Mueller (Grand Rapids: Kregel Publications, 1976), 58.

14 Herndon and Weik, *Herndon's Lincoln*, 359.

Selected Bibliography

Achorn, Edward. *Every Drop of Blood: The Momentous Second Inauguration of Abraham Lincoln.* New York: Atlantic Monthly Press, 2020.

Althusius, Johannes. *Politica.* Translated by Frederick S. Carney. Indianapolis: Liberty Fund, 1995.

Ambrose, Stephen E. *To America: Personal Reflections of an Historian.* New York: Simon & Schuster, 2002.

Ames, William. *The Marrow of Theology.* Translated by John Dykstra Eusden. Grand Rapids: Baker, 1968.

Aquinas, Thomas. "On Kingship." In *From Irenaeus to Grotius: A Sourcebook in Christian Political Thought*, edited by Oliver O'Donovan and Joan Lockwood O'Donovan, 330–41. Grand Rapids and Cambridge, UK: Eerdmans, 1999.

________. "Summa Theologica." *In Introduction to St. Thomas Aquinas,* edited by Anton C. Pegis, 3–428. New York: Random House, 1948.

Ash, Stephen V. *When the Yankees Came: Conflict and Chaos in the Occupied South, 1861–1865.* Chapel Hill: University of North Carolina Press, 1995.

Augustine, *Concerning the City of God against the Pagans.* Translated by Henry Bettenson. London: Penguin, 1984.

________. *Reply to Faustus the Manichaean.* Nicene and Post-Nicene Fathers. Edinburgh: T & T Clark; Grand Rapids: Eerdmans, 1996.

Belz, Herman. "Lincoln, Abraham (1809–65)." In *American Conservatism: An Encyclopedia*, edited by Bruce Frohnen et al, 514–18. Wilmington, DE: ISI Books, 2006.

Beza, Theodore. *Concerning the Rights of Rulers over Their Subjects and the Duty of Subjects toward Their Rulers*. Translated by Henry-Louis Gonin. Capetown and Pretoria: H.A.U.M., 1956.

Blumenthal, Sidney. *All the Powers of the Earth: The Political Life of Abraham Lincoln, 1856–1860*. New York: Simon & Schuster, 2019.

________. *A Self-Made Man: The Political Life of Abraham Lincoln, 1809-1849*. New York: Simon & Schuster, 2016.

________. *Wrestling with His Angel: The Political Life of Abraham Lincoln, 1849–1856*. New York: Simon & Schuster, 2017.

Brookhiser, Richard. *Founders' Son: A Life of Abraham Lincoln*. New York: Basic Books, 2014.

Bucer, Martin. *On the Kingdom of Christ*, edited by Wilhelm Pauck. Philadelphia: Westminster, 1969.

Burke, Edmund. *The Philosophy of Edmund Burke*, edited by Louis Bredvold and Ralph Ross. Ann Arbor: University of Michigan Press, 1960.

Burlamaqui, Jean-Jacques. *The Principles of Natural and Political Law*. Translated by Thomas Nugent. Indianapolis: Liberty Fund, 2006.

Burlingame, Michael. *Abraham Lincoln: A Life*. 2 vols. Baltimore: Johns Hopkins University Press, 2008.

________. *The Black Man's President: Abraham Lincoln, African Americans, & the Pursuit of Racial Equality*. New York and London: Pegasus, 2021.

________. *The Inner World of Abraham Lincoln*. Urbana and Chicago: University of Illinois Press, 1994.

Burlingame, Michael, ed. *An Oral History of Abraham Lincoln: John G. Nicolay's Interviews and Essays*. Carbondale, IL: Southern Illinois Press, 1996.

Burlingame, Michael, and John R. Turner Ettlinger, eds. *Inside Lincoln's White House: The Complete Civil War Diary of John Hay*. Carbondale, IL: Southern Illinois Press, 1997.

Byrd, James P. *A Holy Baptism of Fire and Blood: The Bible and the American Civil War.* New York: Oxford University Press, 2021.

Calvin, John. *Calvin's Commentaries.* Edinburgh: Calvin Translation Society, 1843–55. Reprint. Grand Rapids: Baker, 1979.

________. *Institutes of the Christian Religion.* Translated by Ford Lewis Battles. Philadelphia: Westminster, 1960.

________. Sermon 29. *Sermons on 1 Samuel.* Translated by Douglas F. Kelly. In *Calvin Studies Colloquium.* Davidson, NC: Colloquium on Calvin Studies, 1982.

________. *Sermons on Deuteronomy.* Edinburgh: Banner of Truth, 1987.

________. *Sermons on Titus.* Translated by Robert White. Edinburgh: Banner of Truth, 2015.

Carwardine, Richard. *Lincoln: A Life of Purpose and Power.* New York: Alfred A. Knopf, 2006.

________. *Lincoln's Sense of Humor.* Carbondale, IL: Southern Illinois Press, 2017.

Catton, Bruce. *The American Heritage Short History of the Civil War.* New York: Dell, 1960.

Conforti, Joseph A. *Samuel Hopkins and the New Divinity Movement: Calvinism, the Congregational Ministry, and Reform in New England Between the Great Awakenings.* Eugene, OR: Wipf & Stock, 1981.

Conkin, Paul K. *The Uneasy Center: Reformed Christianity in Antebellum America.* Chapel Hill and London: University of North Carolina Press, 1995.

Dabney, Robert L. "The Christian Soldier." In *Discussions: Evangelical and Theological*, vol. 1, 614–25. Edinburgh: Banner of Truth, 1967.

________. "The Christian's Best Motive for Patriotism." In *Discussions: Evangelical and Theological*, vol. 2, 410–12. Edinburgh: Banner of Truth, 1974.

________. "Christians, Pray for Your Country." In *Discussions: Evangelical and Theological*, vol. 2, 393–400. Edinburgh: Banner of Truth, 1967.

________. "Civic Ethics," in *Discussions: Evangelical and Theological*, vol. 3, 100–26. Edinburgh: Banner of Truth, 1967.

________. *Systematic Theology.* Edinburgh: Banner of Truth, 1985.

Davis, Rodney O., and Douglas L. Wilson, eds. *The Lincoln-Douglas Debates.* Urbana and Chicago: University of Illinois Press, 2008.

D. H. Dilbeck, "'The Sternest Feature of War': The Moral Dilemma of Retaliation and the Limits of Atrocity in the American Civil War." *Fides et Historia* 48, no. 1 (2016): 32–60.

Donald, David Herbert. *Lincoln.* New York: Simon & Schuster, 1995.

________. *"We Are Lincoln Men": Abraham Lincoln and His Friends."* New York: Simon & Schuster, 2003.

Eaton, Clement. *The Growth of Southern Civilization, 1790–1860.* New York: Harper, 1961.

Edwards, Jonathan. "A Strong Rod Broken and Withered." In *The Works of Jonathan Edwards*, vol. 25, edited by Wilson H. Kimnach, 313–30. New Haven: Yale University Press, 2006.

Edwards Jr., Jonathan. "The Injustice and Impolicy of the Slave Trade and of Slavery." In *The New England Theology*, edited by Douglas A. Sweeney and Allen C. Guelzo, 157–64. Eugene, OR: Wipf & Stock, 2015.

________. "The Necessity of the Belief of Christianity." In *Political Sermons of the Founding Era, 1730–1805*, edited by Ellis Sandoz, 1185–1216. Indianapolis: Liberty Press, 1991.

Ellis, Joseph J. *Founding Brothers: The Revolutionary Generation.* New York: Alfred A. Knopf, 2000.

Farmer, James Oscar. *The Metaphysical Confederacy: James Henley Thornwell and the Synthesis of Southern Values.* Macon, GA: Mercer, 1986.

Fehrenbacher, Don E., and Virginia Fehrenbacher, eds. *Recollected Words of Abraham Lincoln.* Stanford: Stanford University Press, 1996.

Fern, Robert L. *Jonathan Edwards the Younger, 1745–1801.* Grand Rapids: Eerdmans, 1976.

Franklin, John H. *The Militant South, 1800–1861.* Cambridge: Harvard University Press, 1956.

Goodwin, Doris Kearns. *Team of Rivals: The Political Genius of Abraham Lincoln.* New York: Simon & Schuster, 2006.

Guelzo, Allen C. *Abraham Lincoln as a Man of Ideas.* Carbondale: Southern Illinois Press, 2009.

________. *Abraham Lincoln: Redeemer President.* Grand Rapids and Cambridge, UK: Eerdmans, 1999.

________. *Fateful Lightning: A History of the Civil War & Reconstruction.* Oxford: Oxford University Press, 2012.

Gundlach, Bradley J. "'Wicked Caste': Warfield, Biblical Authority, and Jim Crow." In *B. B. Warfield: Essays on His Life and Thought*, edited by Gary L. W. Johnson, 136–68. Phillipsburg, NJ: Presbyterian & Reformed, 2007.

Heejoon Jeon. "Jonathan Edwards and the Anti-Slavery Movement." *JETS* 63, no. 4 (2020): 773–88.

Herndon, William H., and Jesse W. Weik. *Herndon's Lincoln*, edited by Douglas L. Wilson and Rodney O. Davis. Urbana and Chicago: University of Illinois Press, 2006.

Hill, John Wesley. *Abraham Lincoln, Man of God.* New York and London: G. P. Putnam's Sons, 1920.

Hodge, Charles. "President Lincoln." *Biblical Repertory and Princeton Review* 37, no. 3 (1865): 435–58.

________. "The Princeton Review on the State of the Country and of the Church." *Biblical Repertory and Princeton Review* 37, no. 4 (1865): 627–57.

Hoffecker, W. Andrew. *Charles Hodge: The Pride of Princeton.* Phillipsburg, NJ: Presbyterian & Reformed, 2011.

Holzer, Harold. *Lincoln and the Power of the Press.* New York: Simon & Schuster, 2014.

________. *Lincoln at Cooper Union: The Speech That Made Abraham Lincoln President.* New York: Simon & Schuster, 2004.

Hopkins, Samuel. "A Dialogue Concerning the Slavery of the Africans, Showing It to Be the Duty and Interest of the American Colonies to Emancipate All Their African Slaves." In *The New England Theology*, edited by Douglas A. Sweeney and Allen C. Guelzo, 151–56. Eugene, OR: Wipf & Stock, 2015.

Howe, Daniel Walker. *The Political Culture of the American Whigs.* Chicago and London: University of Chicago Press, 1979.

Jaffa, Harry V. *A New Birth of Freedom: Abraham Lincoln and the Coming of the Civil War.* Lanham, MD: Rowman & Littlefield, 2000.

________. *Crisis of the House Divided: An Interpretation of the Issues in the Lincoln-Douglas Debates.* Chicago and London: University of Chicago Press, 2009.

John of Salisbury. *Policraticus.* Translated by John Dickinson. New York: Alfred A. Knopf, 1927.

Johnson, James Turner. *Just War Tradition and the Restraint of War: A Moral and Historical Inquiry.* Princeton: Princeton University Press, 1987.

Johnson, Thomas Cary. *The Life and Letters of Benjamin Morgan Palmer.* Richmond, VA: Presbyterian Committee of Publication, 1906.

________. *The Life and Letters of Robert Lewis Dabney*. Edinburgh: Banner of Truth, 1977.

Keegan, John. *The Mask of Command.* New York: Viking, 1987.

Keilor, Steven J. *This Rebellious House: American History and the Truth of Christianity.* Downers Grove, IL: IVP, 1996.

Kendall, Willmore, and George W. Carey. *The Basic Symbols of the American Political Tradition.* Washington, D.C.: Catholic University Press, 1995.

Kingdon, Robert M. *Myths about the St. Bartholomew's Day Massacre, 1572–1576.* Cambridge, MA and London: Harvard University Press, 1988.

Klein, Maury. *Days of Defiance: Sumter, Secession, and the Coming of the Civil War.* New York: Alfred A. Knopf, 1997.

Kull, Irving Stoddard. "Presbyterian Attitudes toward Slavery." *CH* 7, no. 2 (1938): 101–14.

Lincoln, Abraham. "Address at Cooper Institute." In *Lincoln Speeches*, edited by Allen C. Guelzo, 94–102. New York: Penguin, 2012.

________. "Address before the Young Men's Lyceum of Springfield, Illinois." In *Classics of American Political and Constitutional Thought*, vol. 1, edited by Scott J. Hammond et al, 969–73. Indianapolis and Cambridge: Hackett, 2007.

________. "Address to the Washington Temperance Society." In *Lincoln Speeches*, edited by Allen C. Guelzo, 19– 24. New York: Penguin, 2012.

________. "Eulogy on Henry Clay." In *Lincoln Speeches*, edited by Allen C. Guelzo, 32–37. New York: Penguin, 2012.

________. "First Inaugural Address." In *Classics of American Political and Constitutional Thought*, vol. 1, edited by Scott J. Hammond et al, 1085–89. Indianapolis and Cambridge: Hackett, 2007.

———. "Gettysburg Address." In *Classics of American Political and Constitutional Thought*, vol. 1, edited by Scott J. Hammond et al, 1113. Indianapolis and Cambridge: Hackett, 2007.

———. "'House Divided' Speech." In *Lincoln Speeches*, edited by Allen C. Guelzo, 56–63. New York: Penguin, 2012.

———. "Letter to James C. Conkling." In *Lincoln's Speeches*, edited by Allen C. Guelzo, 145–49. New York: Penguin, 2012.

———. "Protest Entered in the Illinois Legislature." In *Lincoln Speeches*, edited by Allen C. Guelzo, 4–5. New York: Penguin, 2012.

———. "Second Inaugural Address." In *Classics of American Political and Constitutional Thought*, vol. 1, edited by Scott J. Hammond et al, 1117–18. Indianapolis and Cambridge: Hackett, 2007.

———. "Speech at Independence Hall." In *Lincoln Speeches*, edited by Allen C. Guelzo, 110–11. New York: Penguin, 2012.

———. "Speech at Peoria." In *Lincoln Speeches*, edited by Allen C. Guelzo, 37–55. New York: Penguin, 2012.

———. "Speech on the 1848 Presidential Race." In *Lincoln Speeches*, edited by Allen C. Guelzo, 27–31. New York: Penguin, 2012.

———. "Speech to the One Hundred Sixty-Six Ohio Regiment." In *Lincoln Speeches*, edited by Allen C. Guelzo, 152–53. New York: Penguin, 2012.

———. "To the People of Sangamo County." In *Lincoln Speeches*, edited by Allen C. Guelzo, 1–4. New York: Penguin, 2012.

Lucas, Sean Michael. *Robert Lewis Dabney: A Southern Presbyterian Life*. Philipsburg, NJ: Presbyterian & Reformed, 2005.

Luther, Martin. "Against the Robbing and Murdering Hordes of Peasants." In *Luther's Works*, vol. 46, edited by Jaroslav Pelikan et al, 45–56. St. Louis: Concordia; Philadelphia: Fortress, 1967.

________. *Commentary on Romans*. Translated by J. Theodore Mueller. Grand Rapids: Kregel, 1976.

________. "On War against the Turk." In *Luther's Works*, vol. 46, edited by Jaroslav Pelikan et al, 155–205. St. Louis: Concordia; Philadelphia: Fortress, 1967.

McDonald, Forrest. *Novus Ordo Seclorum: The Intellectual Origins of the Constitution.* Lawrence, KS: University Press of Kansas, 1985.

McKivigan, John R. *The War against Proslavery Religion: Abolitionism and the Northern Churches, 1830–1865.* Ithaca and London: Cornell University Press, 1984.

McPherson, James M. *Abraham Lincoln.* Oxford: Oxford University Press, 2009.

________. *For Cause and Comrades: Why Men Fought in the Civil War.* New York and Oxford: Oxford University Press, 1997.

Miller, William Lee. *Lincoln's Virtues: An Ethical Biography.* New York: Alfred A. Knopf, 2003.

Minkema, Kenneth P., and Harry S. Stout. "The Edwardsean Tradition and the Antislavery Debate, 1740–1865." *The Journal of American History* 92, no. 1 (2005): 47–74.

Moorhead, James H. *American Apocalypse: Yankee Protestants and the Civil War, 1860–1869.* New Haven and London: Yale University Press, 1978.

Morrill, John. *Oliver Cromwell.* Oxford: Oxford University Press, 2007.

Murray, Iain H. *Jonathan Edwards: A New Biography.* Edinburgh: Banner of Truth, 1987.

Noll, Mark A. *A History of Christianity in the United States and Canada.* Grand Rapids: Eerdmans, 1992.

________. *America's God: From Jonathan Edwards to Abraham Lincoln.* Oxford: Oxford University Press, 2002.

________. *The Civil War as a Theological Crisis.* Chapel Hill: University of North Carolina Press, 2006.

Oates, Stephen B. *Abraham Lincoln: The Man behind the Myths.* New York: Harper & Row, 1984.

Owen, Christopher H. *The Sacred Flame of Love: Methodism and Society in Nineteenth-Century Georgia.* Athens, GA: University of Georgia Press, 1998.

Palmer, Benjamin M. *The Life and Letters of James Henley Thornwell.* Edinburgh: Banner of Truth, 1974.

Rable, George C. *God's Almost Chosen Peoples: A Religious History of the American Civil War.* Chapel Hill: University of North Carolina Press, 2010.

Reilly, Robert R. *America on Trial: A Defense of the Founding.* San Francisco: Ignatius Press, 2020.

Reynolds, David S. *Abe: Abraham Lincoln in His Times.* New York: Penguin, 2020.

Rice, Eugene F., and Anthony Grafton. *The Foundations of Early Modern Europe, 1460–1559.* 2d ed. New York and London: Norton, 1994.

Robertson, James I. *Stonewall Jackson: the Man, the Soldier, the Legend.* New York: Macmillan, 1997.

Sandburg, Carl. *Abraham Lincoln: The Prairie Years.* New York: Charles Scribner's, 1944.

Silver, James W. *Confederate Morale and Church Propaganda.* Tuscaloosa, AL: Confederate Publishing Company, 1957.

Snay, Mitchell. *Gospel of Disunion: Religion and Separatism in the Antebellum South.* Cambridge: Cambridge University Press, 1993.

Stephens, Alexander. "Cornerstone Speech." In *Classics of American Political and Constitutional Thought*, vol. 1, edited by Scott J. Hammond et al, 1090–93. Indianapolis and Cambridge: Hackett, 2007.

Stout, Harry S. *Upon the Altar of the Nation: A Moral History of the Civil War.* New York: Viking, 2006.

Striner, Richard. *Summoned to Glory: The Audacious Life of Abraham Lincoln.* Lanham, MD: Rowman & Littlefield, 2020.

Sweet, William W. *The Story of Religion in America.* New York: Harper, 1950.

Tertullian. "Apology." In *From Irenaeus to Grotius: A Sourcebook in Christian Political Thought*, edited by Oliver O'Donovan and Joan Lockwood O'Donovan, 23–26. Grand Rapids and Cambridge, UK: Eerdmans, 1999.

Thomas, Benjamin P. *Abraham Lincoln: A Biography.* New York: Barnes & Noble, 1952.

Thornwell, James H. "The Christian Doctrine of Slavery." In *The Collected Writings of James Henley Thornwell*, vol. 4, 398–436. Edinburgh: Banner of Truth, 1974.

________. "Relation of the State to Christ." In *The Collected Writings of James Henley* Thornwell, vol. 4, 549–56. Edinburgh: Banner of Truth, 1974.

________. "Sermon on National Sins." In *The Collected Writings of James Henley Thornwell*, vol. 4, 510–48. Edinburgh: Banner of Truth, 1974.

Tyacke, Nicholas. "Puritanism, Arminianism, and Counter-Revolution." In *The Origins of the English Civil War*, edited by Conrad Russell, 119–43. London: Macmillan, 1973.

Warren, Wendy. *New England Bound: Slavery and Colonization in Early America.* New York and London: Liveright, 2016.

White, Ronald C. *A Lincoln: A Biography.* New York: Random House, 2009.

________. *Lincoln in Private: What His Most Personal Reflections Tell Us About Our Greatest President.* New York: Random House, 2021.

________. *Lincoln's Greatest Speech: The Second Inaugural.* New York: Simon & Schuster, 2002.

Widmer, Ted. *Lincoln on the Verge: Thirteen Days to Washington.* New York: Simon & Schuster, 2020.

Williams, T. Harry. *Lincoln and His Generals.* New York: Random House, 1952.

Wilson, Douglas L., and Rodney O. Davis, eds. *Herndon's Informants: Letters, Interviews, and Statements about Abraham Lincoln.* Urbana: University of Illinois Press, 1998.

Wilson, Douglas L. *Honor's Voice: The Transformation of Abraham Lincoln.* New York: Alfred A. Knopf, 1998.

Wills, Garry. *Lincoln at Gettysburg: The Words That Remade America.* New York: Simon & Schuster, 1992.

Wood, Gordon S. *Empire of Liberty: A History of the Early Republic, 1789–1815.* Oxford and New York: Oxford University Press, 2009.

Wood, John Halsey. "The 1861 Spring Resolutions: Charles Hodge, the American Union, and the Dissolution of the Old School Church." *Journal of Church and State* 47, no. 2 (2005): 371–87.

Woodworth, Steven E. *While God Is Marching On: The Religious World of Civil War Soldiers.* Lawrence, KS: University Press of Kansas, 2001.

Wyatt-Brown, Bertram. *Southern Honor: Ethics and Behavior in the Old South.* New York and Oxford: Oxford University Press, 1982.

Zeitz, Joshua. *Lincoln's God: How Faith Transformed a Nation and a President.* New York: Viking, 2023.

Zwingli, Huldrych. *The Defense of the Reformed Faith.* Translated by E. J. Furch. Allison Park, PA: Pickwick, 1984.

Index

Y

Z

About the Author

Mark J. Larson, PhD, majored in biblical studies at Cedarville University and Baptist Bible School of Theology. He studied political theory and international politics at Regent University. He earned a ThM in systematic theology at Westminster Theological Seminary and a PhD in historical theology at Calvin Theological Seminary.

He is the author of *Abraham Kuyper, Conservatism, and Church and State* (2015) and *Calvin's Doctrine of the State: A Reformed Doctrine and Its American Trajectory, the Revolutionary War, and the Founding of the Republic* (2009). He is the co-author of *The Reformers on War, Peace, and Justice* (2019).

He has contributed to *War and Religion: An Encyclopedia of Faith and Conflict*; *Biblical Interpretation and Doctrinal Formulation in the Reformed Tradition*; and *Church and School in Early Modern Protestantism*. He has been published in several peer-reviewed journals—*Westminster Theological Journal*; *Scottish Bulletin of Evangelical Theology*; *Bibliotheca Sacra*; *Journal of Presbyterian History*; *Reformation and Renaissance Review*; *Journal of Dispensational Theology*; *Detroit Baptist Seminary Journal*; *Foundations: An International Journal of Evangelical Theology*; and *Puritan Reformed Journal*. His articles have appeared in *The Banner of Truth*, *The Outlook*, *New Horizons*, and *Christian Renewal*. He has served as a high school teacher, pastor, and seminary professor.